What people a

Conform or Be Cast Out

Modernity was born with the advent of liberalism, and that in turn rested on one major insight: people who are different, who disagree, can coexist and build a beautiful civilization. No need to burn heretics or cast out people based on belief systems or other arbitrary categories. Human dignity can be universal. It's remarkable to me that we would need to restate these points, but we do, which is precisely why Logan Albright's book is so essential. Conformity is not the basis of social order; rather we need tolerance, robust debate, and mutual respect. That's not a radical proposition, except that these days it is. Albright's clarion call to recommit to fundamental values strikes all the right notes.
Jeffrey Tucker, American Institute for Economic Research

We humans can be creatures of habit. On most decisions, mundane to monumental, we mindlessly comply with the rules of civil society without giving it a second thought. But then again, there are the troublemakers. The rule-breakers. Those pesky free thinkers impolitic enough to ask: "Why?" Logan Albright's latest book is an unapologetic celebration of these eccentric oddballs, and all of the beautiful things that might happen when free people refuse to fall in line. Read it, and you just might unleash your inner apostate.
Matt Kibbe, Author of *Don't Hurt People and Don't Take Their Stuff: A Libertarian Manifesto*

An informed discussion of the trials and tribulations of being an individual – both across history and mythology – a suitable introduction to the problems of the modern technological age.
Mark Stavish, Founder, Institute for Hermetic Studies

Conform or Be Cast out

The (Literal) Demonization of Nonconformists

Conform or Be Cast out

The (Literal) Demonization
of Nonconformists

Logan Albright

MOON
BOOKS

Winchester, UK
Washington, USA

JOHN HUNT PUBLISHING

First published by Moon Books, 2021
Moon Books is an imprint of John Hunt Publishing Ltd., No. 3 East Street, Alresford
Hampshire SO24 9EE, UK
office@jhpbooks.net
www.johnhuntpublishing.com
www.moon-books.net

For distributor details and how to order please visit the 'Ordering' section on our website.

Text copyright: Logan Albright 2020

ISBN: 978 1 78904 842 1
978 1 78904 843 8 (ebook)
Library of Congress Control Number: 2020950151

A CIP catalogue record for this book is available from the British Library.

Design: Stuart Davies

UK: Printed and bound by CPI Group (UK) Ltd, Croydon, CR0 4YY
Printed in North America by CPI GPS partners

We operate a distinctive and ethical publishing philosophy in all areas of our business, from our global network of authors to production and worldwide distribution.

Contents

Also by Logan Albright

Our Servants, Our Masters: How Control Masquerades as Assistance

ISBN 9781630691882

Acknowledgments

I wish to thank everyone at John Hunt Publishing and Moon Books for their support of this project, Matt and Terry Kibbe for the freedom and encouragement to write books even when others think it's a waste of time, and all the members of the Firefly House for helping me along on my continuing spiritual quest. Of course, I extend my deepest gratitude to my loving parents for offering me their unwavering support in all my creative endeavors, however quixotic.

Introduction

Humans are social animals. We live in groups, we cooperate, we form communities, we help each other, all in the name of making life better. But as G.K. Chesterton was fond of pointing out, humans are also contradictions. For all our love of community and social activity, we are also individuals, each with our own thoughts, feelings, preferences, philosophies, and opinions about the world. It is this tension between the individual and the communal that continues to drive much political debate in the United States, and indeed around the world. On the one side, you have the individualists, the libertarians, the free thinkers, the nonconformists, under which category the present author, in the interest of full disclosure, must admit to falling. On the other side, you have the collectivists, the nationalists, the socialists, the communists, and those who believe that the bonds of community and charity must be prioritized above individual rights or welfare, by force if necessary.

Much to the dismay of people like myself, for the last several thousand years, the collectivists have been winning, and one of the reasons they have been winning is their overwhelming superiority at using language and storytelling to reinforce their worldview among the undecided. They do so with such skill that most people don't even realize that their thinking is being manipulated. Think of the word "selfish" and what comes to mind? Someone who treats others badly, and who is likely to lie, cheat, and steal to get what he wants. In reality, the self is a wonderful thing that should not be neglected, but should be nurtured and developed to the maximum of its potential. But subtle collectivist thinking has, over time, given the word an intensely negative connotation. The author and philosopher Ayn Rand tried to point this out numerous times in her writings, but due to the clumsiness of much of her philosophical writing, her message came out garbled to all but the most devoted readers willing to work hard enough to figure out what she really meant.

Collectivist messaging can be found pretty much anywhere we care to look for it, but perhaps the most audacious example, and the focus of this book, is the way in which individualists, nonconformists, and people who refuse to do as they're told by the rest of society, have so frequently throughout history been demonized. The word, as it is most commonly used, is strictly metaphorical. To demonize someone is to paint them as a bad actor, as someone with malevolent motives, or at the very least as someone acting against the common interest of society. We see metaphorical demonization every day in politics, in current events, in religion, in polemical writing of all types. Indeed, it's hard to find any public figure who is not, to some degree or other, demonized on a regular basis. You can be sure, however, that the bulk of the bile and hatred society has to muster is lobbed in the direction of those who are a bit different than the rest. The people who hold unpopular opinions, live unconventional lives, refuse to do as they're told, and fail to toe the party line risk not only public censure and vilification, but often death threats and actual attacks on their person as well.

Demonization in the metaphorical sense is far too common to be the subject of a book that has any hope of being coherently organized. A history of demonization would encompass the entire history of the world. But there is a specific subcategory of demonization that seems wholly fitting for in-depth study. I'm referring, of course, to demonization in its original, most literal sense. By this I mean that, on multiple occasions and through a variety of movements across the centuries, the powers that be, whether housed in the church, the secular government, or merely people in positions of great influence, have classified nonconformists as being, or else acting in the service of, *actual demons.*

It sounds so extreme that it's hard to believe, and it's equally hard to believe that society as a whole would be willing to swallow such obvious propaganda, and yet it happened, again and again, not only in primitive, superstitious backwaters, but shockingly recently in our own country. In some ways, it still continues today.

Before moving on, I should clarify that I am not arguing that all nonconformity is necessarily good. Murder, rape, theft, and other kinds of violence are all acts which cut sharply against the established mores of society, and these are obviously terrible crimes which should be discouraged and condemned in the strongest possible terms. But even though certain types of nonconformity are destructive to peaceful living, other types can be either harmless or downright advantageous. After all, it has always been the oddballs, the weirdos, the trend-buckers, the eccentrics, and even the so-called madmen who are responsible for the truly great breakthroughs in art, music, science, and philosophy. Without nonconformity, there could be no advancement. Everyone would just go on doing things the way they have always been done, and no one would have the drive or self-confidence necessary to upset the proverbial apple cart in search of some tastier fruit.

If this is the case, which it pretty obviously is, why then should society at large be so quick to condemn those who march to the beat of their own drum? It is likely that the answer can be found in the dingy backwater of prehistory, when continued existence depended on small tribes of people working together in order to solve the extremely difficult problems of how to get enough food to eat while not being themselves eaten by predators. The famous libertarian economist Friedrich Hayek, in his final book entitled *The Fatal Conceit*, devotes a good deal of space to exploring this notion. The collectivist impulse, he argues, is embedded deeply in the human psyche, because it is through collectivism that we emerged out of the primordial soup of life and into something vaguely resembling civilization.

When people live in very small groups, say a family or a tribe, it is advantageous to work as a unit. There is no private property within the nuclear family, but everything is shared and employed towards the primary goal of keeping the family alive and well. In tribes, there is a chief and everyone does what the chief says, for the good of the tribe. A nonconformist in a group of individuals trying to function as a coherent unit tends to gum up the works, just like a rogue spring or gear would utterly destroy the mechanism of a finely-tuned watch. Everything has to function in concert, or else the whole thing falls apart, and so nonconformity must be punished, and severely, lest the family or tribe suffer as a result.

This collectivist system works pretty well, but only for the reason that, in a small group, everyone can be held accountable. If someone shirks their duty, it is immediately obvious to all involved, and corrective action can be taken. But when you expand the group size past a certain point, this system is no longer tenable. In a large society, it becomes impossible to know every individual member on a personal level, and therefore it is impossible to know whether everyone is following the plan to the best of his ability. It's impossible to know what people are really capable of, what their needs are, who's shirking, who's legitimately in need of help, and who's trying to game the system to secure maximum benefit for himself. As accountability breaks down, so does the central plan as designed by the chief. The collective system of the tribe must give way to a market system where individuals pursuing their own interests create a functioning society without even meaning to. This is what Adam Smith called the Invisible Hand of the marketplace, a spontaneously generated system that allows for individual action with little to no need for group identity.

In a market system, the nonconformist no longer threatens to bring the whole machine crashing down. Someone who acts strangely or unpredictably may ruin his own life, to be sure, or he may stumble upon unimagined riches and success. He takes the risk, and he bears the consequences, and if he fails, there are thousands more like him to keep society running.

Yet, throughout this restructuring of society from small tribes to complex cities, we have carried with us that primal distrust and fear for those who refuse to live their lives in a conventional way, and far from reveling in the diversity that markets allow, too many of us still seek to squash disobedience good and hard. The best way to do that, it turns out, is to represent difference itself as the literal stuff of nightmares. Use fear to bring people in line; it's the oldest trick in the book, probably because it still works after all these years.

In the following chapters, I hope to demonstrate how nonconformists have been consistently represented as the servants of Darkness through the centuries, and how even today we continue to hold onto attitudes demonizing those who wish to live, love, and work in unfamiliar ways. It may be that through greater understanding of this phenomenon, we can start to let go of some of the fear we feel towards the nonconformists, and start to treat them with the tolerance, and indeed fascination they deserve.

Chapter 1

From Serpent To Satan

When discussing a topic that spans much of human history, it can be difficult to know where to begin. There have been nonconformists for as long as there have been human beings with complex societies, and this certainly goes back to the invention of writing, if not even further. I could try to find the first example of a nonconformist in history or literature and see how society treated that individual, or I could try to find the first example of a nonconformist being punished for his actions. Instead, I'm going to take the easy way out by starting at the beginning, as defined by the most influential book in western culture, The Bible.

The Book of Genesis, and especially the story of the Garden of Eden is well known to almost everyone in the Western world. God created the first man, Adam, and the first woman, Eve, and plopped them down in paradise to do whatever they wanted, with one major exception. Whatever you do, God commands, don't eat from this one tree planted in the center of the garden, the Tree of the Knowledge of Good and Evil. All the other trees are fine, but don't touch *that* one.

Of course, as soon as God turns his back, a serpent appears and convinces Eve that her interests run contrary to God's commandment, and that eating from the tree would make Adam and Eve more like gods themselves. God is just holding them back as helpless dependents out of spite. Eve is quickly convinced, and she and Adam eat from the tree. Immediately, they realize that they are naked, feel ashamed, and seek to cover themselves with makeshift clothing. God comes back and finds out that his orders have been disobeyed, and after a stern lecture, kicks Adam and Eve out of the garden. That's why life is hard, bearing children is painful, and snakes don't have any legs, apparently.

That's a simple enough moral: do as you're told; don't try to rise above your station; don't listen to talking snakes. Nonconformity is punished in the swiftest and most terrible fashion, and the serpent, the tempter, is primarily to blame, but we'll get back to him in a minute.

Another story from early Judaism, though less well known, carries a similar moral. According to some scholars, Eve was not the original wife of Adam, nor the first created woman. She was a second attempt after the first one, called Lilith, went wrong.

In the myth of Lilith, the first wife of Adam, it is told that she was created independently of Adam, unlike Eve who was created from the rib of Adam. Thus, Lilith did not want to submit to Adam, something that led to an argument regarding who should lie underneath during sex. Finally, God had to intervene and he attempted to force Lilith to submit to Adam. But Lilith spoke the secret name of God, Shemhamforash, and managed to escape. She escaped out of the Garden of Eden into the wild lands where she encountered demons, like Samael and Asmodeus.[1]

Nowadays, Lilith is generally referred to as a demon herself, queen of the vampires, and mother of all dark and evil things. Her crime? Once again, it is nothing more than disdain for authority, nonconformity to the expectations of others, and a refusal to allow herself to be dominated. These generally admirable traits are literally demonized in the story of Lilith, leading to her becoming an adopted mascot in some circles of modern feminism.

Before moving on, it's important to note that warnings against disobeying the gods were nothing new, nor were they unique to Judaism. The mythology of the ancient Greeks is full of cautionary tales about what happens when humans fail to live up to divine expectations. This is not surprising, given the fact that gods were, by definition, powerful, being the forces behind nature itself and causing everything from lightning and earthquakes to wars and even love. It's only natural to fear and obey something that has the power to reduce your village to ash, or worse, to make you fall in love with someone who doesn't love you back. But to the Greeks, at least, obedience was not necessarily seen as inherently virtuous, just prudent.

To the ancient Greeks, the gods were to be honored and obeyed not because they were good, but because they were powerful. They could make your life better, or they could ruin you without even trying, so it was best to stay on their good side. By the same token, however, if you could manage to pull one over on the gods and get away with it, more power to you. Zeus, Hades, and Ares were not heroes to be loved and adored. They were just as ruthless and petty as any human warlord. This is why there are plenty of stories of particularly crafty humans, and sometimes non-humans, beating the gods at their own game, and the best of these stories is that of Prometheus.

Prometheus was a Titan, the Titans being a race that preceded and were ultimately conquered by Zeus and the other gods of Mount Olympus. Prometheus was uncommonly sympathetic to human kind, having observed the way they struggled to eke out an existence, and he figured that they could use a little help from above. Noting the usefulness of divine fire, one day Prometheus took it upon himself to give humans the gift of fire making, allowing them heat in the cold, light in the dark, and finally some decently cooked food to eat. When Zeus learned what Prometheus had done, he was furious. Fire was one of the gods' main advantages over the humans, and with a single action, Prometheus had elevated an inferior race one step closer to Mount Olympus. As punishment, the poor Titan was chained to a rock and doomed to have his liver eaten by eagles, only to have it grow back to be pecked out and devoured again and again forever. It would be hard to imagine a worse punishment for any crime, much less the relatively minor one of actually helping humans not die of exposure or starvation, but the Greek gods were never exactly models of restraint or mercy.

Why do I tell this story? Because, as you may have noticed, it bears a striking resemblance to the story of the serpent in the Garden of Eden. Someone breaks ranks and reveals forbidden knowledge to mankind, which is great for them but angers the gods who had been jealously guarding these secrets. The act of disobedience, of refusal to conform, is subsequently punished in the harshest possible terms, and the rest of us are expected to learn from the example and never, ever do it again.

The crucial difference between the Garden of Eden and Prometheus stories is this: Prometheus was regarded as a hero by the Greeks. He risked everything to help us out, and paid the price. What a guy. And if you are feeling sorry for him, you can take comfort in the fact that, spoiler alert, he eventually gets rescued by Hercules, presumably because the Greeks found his torment an intolerable miscarriage of justice. All's well that ends well.

So, if Prometheus is considered to be awesome for defying the gods and giving us the forbidden knowledge of fire, why is the serpent considered wicked for defying God and giving us the forbidden knowledge of good and evil?

The difference is this: to the Hebrews, God wasn't just powerful, he was also the embodiment of all things good, just and wise. There was no use trying to cheat him, because in the end you were only cheating yourself. Therefore, any disobedience to God's will was regarded as *per se* wicked, and was condemned as such. When the serpent tempts Eve to eat from the Tree of the Knowledge of Good and Evil, this is regarded not as a heroic act, but as a base one. Instead of reveling in this triumph over authority, we are supposed to feel shame and regret. Adam and Eve are cast out from their childlike state of innocence and dependence, and made to suffer the pain and toil of life as independent adults in an inhospitable world. And what was their crime, deserving of such rough treatment? Eve was guilty of curiosity and disobedience. Adam was guilty of putting his faith in another human being, the woman he loved, instead of in a distant authority figure. Thus, in the first few pages of the scriptures that define much of Western civilization, we are taught that there is no greater evil than to question authority.

It's impossible to read the Old Testament without noticing the intense focus on tribalism, insularity, and xenophobia. The early Hebrews were a tribal people, and the laws laid down in the Hebrew Bible were intended for the tribe of Israel, God's chosen people. These laws were at best indifferent and at worst actively hostile to outsiders. Numerous commentators have pointed out Biblical injunctions encouraging slavery, conquest, and genocide of foreigners and heathens. The Ten Commandments prohibiting theft, murder, and other vices, were meant to govern conduct within the tribe only.

In fact, the Old Testament is filled with commandments, far more than just the ten most people are familiar with, that are designed to enforce conformity within the tribe. The Book of Leviticus forbids tattoos, shaving off one's beard, certain haircuts, and certain types of cloth. Dietary laws made sure that everyone ate the same food, and deviant sexual practices are strictly outlawed. All this is understandable within the context in which such rules were written. In addition to providing practical guidelines for harmonious living, these commandments allowed the Jewish people to establish a unique identity within a complex landscape of warring tribes, and helped draw a distinction between in-group and out-group. Avoiding pork and shellfish would cut down on food borne illness and avoiding homosexuality would encourage rapid reproduction within the tribe, but prohibitions on hairstyles and tattoos expressly targeted visible indicators of non-Jewish religious practices. The prohibition against "rounding off the corners of your beard" seems puzzlingly worded, unless you understand the reference to circular hairstyles in competing tribes designed to mimic, and thereby exalt, the shape of the sun. Sun worship is likely the oldest form of religion, and the authors of Leviticus wanted to be clear that, while that sort of thing might be good enough for their neighbors, Yahweh was having none of it.

As a tribal structure with Yahweh as its commander-in-chief, it's not surprising that the tribal mindset of collectivism and conformity was dominant among the early Hebrews, nor that this mindset was carried over into Christianity in the first century. In order for small groups of persecuted peoples to survive and prosper in a hostile world, group cohesion would have been of supreme importance. The early Christian sects were in as much danger of being stamped out or enslaved as the Jews, so it makes sense for those attitudes to migrate to the new faith.

Additionally, the more or less new mindset that God is infinitely merciful, good, and forgiving added a new element of morality to conformity. Eccentric individuals were not just acting against the group interest. They were opposing divine will. And if divine will is good by definition, then anyone who opposes it must be equivalently evil. Thus, the concept of heresy and the need to punish heretics. More on that in a later chapter.

Carl Jung, the Swiss psychologist, elaborates on this idea in his short work *Answer to Job:*

This was the essential difference between Yahweh and the all-ruling Father Zeus, who in a benevolent and somewhat detached manner allowed the economy of the universe to roll along on its accustomed courses and punished only those who were disorderly. He did not moralize but ruled purely instinctively. He did not demand anything more from human beings than the sacrifices due to him; he did not want to do anything with *human beings because he had no plans for them. Father Zeus is certainly a figure but not a personality. Yahweh, on the other hand, was interested in man. Human beings were a matter of first-rate importance for him. He needed them as they needed him, urgently and personally. Zeus too could throw thunderbolts about, but only at hopelessly disorderly individuals. Against mankind as a whole he had no objections — but then they did not interest him all that much. Yahweh, on the other hand, could get inordinately excited about man as a species and men as individuals if they did not behave as he desired or expected, without considering that in his omnipotence he could easily have created something better than these 'bad earthenware pots.'*[2]

Perhaps by coincidence, the evolution of man's conception of God from capricious to wise and benevolent provided a solution to a major problem for early civilization. A person who deviated from their expected behavior could easily weaken, or even actively endanger a small, close-knit community. It was important for the group to enforce conformity and discourage deviant behavior. Threats of physical violence will accomplish this to a certain extent, but this solution has the dual problem of creating resentment against the enforcers and egging on those who are rebellious by nature. Just as we now know that spankings and beatings are largely ineffective ways to get children to behave, threats to expel or even kill nonconformists were not the ideal way to maintain a productive and happy tribe.

People tend to be stubborn and difficult, and the only real way to get them to do what you want is if they also want the same thing. True change can only come from within. By presenting an act of disobedience as contrary to God's perfect plan, it was suddenly possible to instill feelings of shame and guilt into the nonconformist, while simultaneously uniting the rest of the group against him. The added threat of hellfire for wrongdoing created a powerful emotional and spiritual incentive for would-be rebels to behave themselves.

Once you have a divine will that is perfectly righteous and good, it is a short road to start visualizing its opposite. Again, the concept of demons, beings responsible for misfortune, illness, death, and so on, predates Christianity or even Judaism. But traditional demons were disorganized, decentralized, and more often than not a simple personification of natural forces common in animistic religions. The concept of a single demonic force embodying all the evil in the world sprang out of the monotheistic conception of a single source for goodness, with its opposite necessarily being a single source of badness. In a word, the Devil.

It's worth noting that the serpent in Genesis was not originally regarded as "the Devil." He was just a cunning, sneaky serpent that happened to be able to talk, much like the kind we would expect to find in one of Aesop's fables. Only with the development of Christianity did the serpent become synonymous with Satan, the father of all lies. And it's no wonder, for who else could be responsible for the fall of all mankind into original sin, death, and potential damnation? In fact, the development of Lucifer into the embodiment of all things evil has proven handy in a number of ways, making anything undesirable instantly comprehensible as the product of Satan's dark machinations. Retroactively identifying him with the serpent is just the most prominent instance of using the Prince of Darkness' name as a stamp of disapproval.

Given the Bible's overwhelming popularity, and given its unique twist on a more or less classic myth where the hero (Prometheus) becomes the villain (Satan), it's safe to say that the story of the Garden of Eden was a major driving factor in the subsequent four thousand or so years of not just punishing nonconformity, not just disapproving of it, but of identifying the nonconforming individual as something resembling an actual demon.

Scapegoats

All of the stories so far related have something in common: they single out an individual as the source for a complex problem. After all, when something goes wrong, there must be someone to blame. There must be a comprehensible target for finger-pointing. The idea that bad things sometimes just happen for no reason was too much for early man—and generally for modern man as well—to fathom. Thus, Eve's disobedience is to blame for women's pain in childbirth and man's difficulty in scratching a living out of the unforgiving soil. The serpent's temptation is to blame for Eve's transgression. Satan is to blame for all lies, tricks, and misfortunes, however natural their origin may seem.

We can learn something about this tendency by examining the ancient custom of scapegoating. Here again, we use the term in a metaphorical sense today, but originally it meant something far more literal. A tribe who had been visited by bad luck or a run of misfortunes would select a goat and symbolically burden it with all the sins of the village. The goat would then be driven away into the wilderness, in the hope that it would take all the tribe's wickedness with it, leaving nothing behind to inspire the anger of the gods.

Sir James Frazer, a nineteenth century anthropologist and one of the first Europeans to earnestly attempt to conduct a systematic study of world folklore and mythology, goes into considerable detail about this practice in his monumental, though now outdated work, *The Golden Bough.* He points out that in addition to livestock, many cultures would attempt to send evil away in a boat or other inanimate object, while others would select a human for this same purpose.

In ancient Rome, Frazer tells us, a man was dressed in animal skins, beaten with rods, and driven out of the city every March to cast out the collective evils of his peers. In ancient Greece, a slave was beaten and driven away to ward off hunger, and when plague reared its ugly head, a poor man would volunteer to take on the sickness, be driven out of town, and allow himself to be stoned to death. Why would anyone agree to such a humiliating and painful end? It's difficult to say, but apart from a sense of duty and custom, it's worth noting that before the fatal ceremony such a volunteer would be treated with great honor and style at the public expense, being well fed, dressed in finery, and generally treated like a king by those who stood to benefit from his sacrifice.

This is all part of Frazer's broader study of "slaying the god", which is the central focus of his book, and into which we needn't delve too deeply. For our purposes, it's sufficient to note that the people selected to be scapegoats and the bearers of sin and misfortune were not treated as ordinary or representative of the population as a whole. They were singled out as special, either by serving as a symbolic god or simply through the costumes and luxurious treatment afforded them. The same can be said for the animals sacrificed in this way, which were held to be more than simple barnyard creatures, but were rendered singular through the process of selection and expulsion from the tribe. In other words, scapegoats must necessarily be special, different, and separate from the broader population whose welfare they are supposed to safeguard, even if that specialness has to be artificially conferred upon them through ceremony. An ordinary, obedient, and conforming individual would no doubt be wholly unsuitable for such a punishment.[3]

The same principle can be found in operation in instances of human or animal sacrifices designed to please the gods and ward off misfortune. An individual is selected and punished, not for any individual transgressions he may have committed, but to absolve the collective of guilt and, hopefully, prevent divine retribution. It may also have been an easy way to promote group solidarity by doing away with any pesky troublemakers who refused to do as they were told, although this is far from clear in the literature.

Chapter 2

Paradise Lost

The belief in demons and evil spirits is probably as old as humanity itself, but the notion of a single, dominant entity overseeing and responsible for all wickedness in the world didn't really exist until the birth of Christianity. Before that, there were certainly fearful gods of death and darkness, trickster figures, and rulers of the underworld. But although Hades may have been scary, he was also regarded as a necessary part of the divine order. Like a mortician or gravedigger, he had a dirty job, but somebody had to do it. Tricksters like Loki or Pan got up to plenty of mischief, to be sure, but they were not necessarily malicious and occasionally they would actually end up helping mankind by pulling one over on the other gods. These were basically agents of chaos (Pan, for example, gives us the word "panic"), and while chaos may not be exactly desirable, neither is it uniformly evil either. If it were, it would no longer be chaos. In the Old Testament, you can find scattered references to Lucifer, the Morning Star, fallen angels, and demons. But the Hebrews didn't really believe in a Hell, *per se*. The concept of Sheol, the Jewish land of the dead, was closer to the Greek notion of the underworld as rather dark and depressing, but neither tortuous nor inherently evil. The demons mentioned in the Old Testament are mainly the gods of neighboring tribes, presented as wicked in order to comply with the First Commandment: "Thou shalt have no other gods before me".

It is only in the New Testament where we start to hear Jesus talk of Satan, a word which translates loosely as "adversary." Satan, Jesus tells us, is the being responsible for tempting us to sin. He rules Hell, which is a place so terrible it is akin to being cast into a lake of fire (whether or not it is a literal lake of fire depends on which Christians you ask.)

Satan is not really described in the Bible, although the Book of Revelation has a number of colorful word-paintings that read more like the product of a vivid and terrifying hallucination than an attempt at an accurate anatomical representation of the Prince of Darkness. But Satan is, understandably, a fascinating figure and as such he became quite popular as a subject for art and literature. He therefore needed to be represented in some sort of physical form. The popular image of Satan we're used to today, complete with horns, cloven hooves, and a tail, was largely derived from identification with pagan and heathen gods the early Christians wanted to discourage people from worshipping. Many of these religions had a tendency to anthropomorphize gods in the shape of animals that were familiar to them, so from Pan the devil took on goat legs and hooves. From Cernunnos, the horned god from Celtic mythology, the devil derived his horns. The tail could have come from any number of places, but as a major distinguishing feature between man and beast, it makes a lot of sense, symbolically.

Over the years, Satan has been represented in a wide variety of ways. He can be seen as incorporeal or metaphorical, as the animalistic demon described above, or as a debonair and charming upper-class gentleman, whose persuasiveness is his greatest weapon. In one particularly good episode of the *Twilight Zone*, he's depicted as a jolly, corpulent man in a business suit going by the ridiculous name of Cadwallader. But far and away my favorite description of the devil is the one developed by John Milton is his epic poem, *Paradise Lost*.

Milton was already a celebrated poet, as well as an advocate for free speech and political liberalism before composing his greatest work. He authored love poems and morality plays. Like Shakespeare before him, he coined dozens of words and phrases still in common use in English today. At a certain point, Milton began to lose his eyesight, and by the time he started work on *Paradise Lost*, he was completely blind. He dictated the poem to his daughter, claiming divine inspiration as the reason he was able to produce page after page of elegant iambic pentameter without apparent effort. Regardless of the source of his inspiration, the final product is a work of genius, one of the finest poems of the English language, and influential beyond belief in our modern conception of Hell and, yes, the Devil himself.

Paradise Lost opens with the end of a war in Heaven, instigated by Satan and a number of other renegade angels who, dissatisfied with God's rule, wanted to shake things up. Unsurprisingly, the rebels lose (God is called God for a reason, after all) and as punishment are cast down into a lake of fire, surrounded by the dark and lonely caverns of Hell itself. After a period of recuperation, Satan builds a capital city called Pandemonium in Hell, rallies his followers and resolves to make the most of his misfortune. Eventually, he escapes Hell, learns of God's plan to create mankind, disguises himself as a snake, slithers his way into the Garden of Eden, and tempts Eve to eat the fruit of the Tree of the Knowledge of Good and Evil. We know the rest.

This story is not particularly unique; most of it appears in the Bible, as we have already seen. But what makes Milton's poem so special is that the story is told from Satan's point of view, and surprisingly for a text written in the seventeenth century in heavily Christian Europe, the Devil is actually portrayed with a fair degree of sympathy.

The most famous line in the poem will be familiar to many readers, Satan's quip that it is "better to reign in Hell than serve in Heaven." Usually this is interpreted as a lust for power at any cost, but in context it reads somewhat differently. Satan makes a compelling case in the poem that he and his fellow angels in Heaven were treated as slaves without the freedom of choice that distinguishes mankind from the immortals. He argues that the hard liberty of his blasted existence is preferable to the comfortable captivity of living out eternity as an indentured servant to the divine, a position remarkably similar to revolutionaries and refugees throughout all history who threw off tyranny in favor of an uncertain and often painful freedom.

In an effort to make the protagonist of his poem relatable, Milton appears to have accidentally painted him as a hero. This has been pointed out by other writers and critics, most notably Phillip Pullman, author of the *His Dark Materials* trilogy, who has written extensive praise and analysis of the poem. It has been said that Milton "was of the Devil's party without realizing it" and it would seem that no one else at the time realized it either. As far as I can tell, *Paradise Lost* was never regarded as heretical nor condemned by the Vatican or any other church. It was, and still is, celebrated as a document affirming the principles of Christianity. Indeed, the church seemed to regard it as self-evident that Milton's characterization of Lucifer as noble, self-sufficient, independent, rebellious, and free thinking confirmed rather than contradicted his role as the father of all evil. Just like with the story of Adam and Eve, the crime worthy of ultimate punishment was a refusal to conform and a desire for individual freedom, an escape from the paternalistic clutches of a disciplinarian deity.

Satan's crime, for which he must suffer the ultimate punishment, is the same as Eve's: disobedience. Once again, the moral of the story is "do as you're told." But unlike Eve, Lucifer does not merely suffer a punishment, but is described as an active source of evil, spreading lies, deceit, trickery, pain, and misery wherever he goes. It's a pretty convenient device to isolate bad behavior by claiming that the transgressor is so wicked that even his mere presence should be avoided at all costs. What better way to prevent the spread of dangerous or nonconforming ideas than with a quarantine enforced by fear? In the middle ages, logic itself was condemned as a product of Satan's tricks, when scientists, then known as natural philosophers, began to question official church positions. When merely asking questions and examining evidence is regarded as demonic, you know that something fishy is going on.

The Devil is repeatedly described as a liar and a tempter, preemptively rendering any statement by him (or by those claimed to be in his employ) suspicious and untrustworthy. In short, good boys and girls are instructed not to use their own minds to decipher truth from falsehood, but to automatically trust authority and distrust everything else. Conform, and don't ask questions.

It's not surprising that Milton was the source for this subtly iconoclastic view of Lucifer. He himself was a bit of a radical and a free thinker, having penned a lengthy defense of the free press against a censorious monarchy called *Areopagitica*. He also boldly wrote on the subject of regicide, the removal of an unfit or tyrannical monarch by killing, in a time when such ideas were dangerous even to think, much less write down.

In the foreword to a collection of Milton's political writings, John Alvis highlights the poet's tendency towards nonconformity throughout his life:

> *Milton's life as a religious controversialist parallels his changing affiliations in political controversy. The young man destined, as he thought, for the clergy, first made common cause with the Anglicans against papist oppression. "Church-Outed" by his refusal to subscribe to oaths of conformity, Milton subsequently joined the Presbyterians in their repudiation of the episcopal form or Protestantism only to break with John Knox's sect when it became clear that the Presbyterians meant to establish another national church. During the Civil War, Milton initially found his party with the Independents, but eventually he ceased to hold communion with any sect and ended by constituting himself a church of one, professing the unique theology worked out in his posthumously published* The Christian Doctrine."[4]

Milton himself, though avoiding prosecution for his potentially heretical views, appears to have received little in the way of respect as a reward for his nonconformity. After being paid the paltry sum of £20 for *Paradise Lost*, he died in impoverished emaciation and was given a poor burial. In her rather strange book, *English Eccentrics*, Edith Sitwell relates the story of how Milton's body was unceremoniously exhumed, his bones, teeth, and hair harvested by interested parties, and distributed as relics. That the remains of one of England's greatest poets should be so ill-used is unfortunate, but perhaps not surprising given the lasting impact of his life's work on diabolism.

That the story of *Paradise Lost* has endured and remains one of the most celebrated classics of English poetry says a lot about the archetypes and themes Milton employed to create an essentially relatable drama. To dismiss his sympathetic portrayal of the Devil as unintentional seems an insult to his genius; on the other hand, we must admit that he was faced with some inherent difficulties in the source material not easily overcome by even the greatest poet.

In essence, the leaders of the Christian Church face the same problem that writers of Superman comics have been struggling with for seventy years, and probably the reason why Hollywood has failed to produce a definitive film version of the Man of Steel. The problem is this: how do you make an omnipotent super-being sympathetic to an audience of fallible, sinful humans? Without weaknesses, there are no challenges for the hero, no obstacles to be overcome, no learning, no growth. God, in the Christian understanding, is already perfect, so there's nowhere for him to go as a character, and unlike Superman he doesn't have kryptonite to knock him down every once in a while.

Milton's Lucifer, on the other hand, is the ultimate underdog. Sure, he's got his problems, but he took on the most powerful being in the universe in the name of freedom and independence. You have to admit, that takes guts. Ironically, it echoes another biblical story, albeit with the roles reversed. Satan here plays the role of David to God's Goliath. If courage, self-sacrifice, and continuing to struggle in spite of overwhelming adversity are virtues, then it's hard not to perceive at least some element of the heroic in Milton's anti-hero, who willingly trades in a life of easy comfort for an eternity of suffering and oppression in order to be his own person.

As a story, it bears marked similarities to the colonization of the American continent and the establishment of the United States as an independent nation. Early pilgrims left behind all that they knew and loved for the chance at a fresh start in a hostile untamed wilderness where safety was most definitely not guaranteed. One can only imagine the courage it must have taken to embark on a six-week ocean voyage with nothing at the other end but forest, mountains, and an indigenous population that might very well decide to kill you for intruding onto their land.

Later, after the colonies had been firmly established, Americans were again willing to gamble their lives in a crazy, hopeless war against the most powerful military in the world. Why? Because the taxes on tea were too high. It was an effort that would rightly be regarded as arrogance bordering on lunacy, were it not for the simple fact that it happened to work. Even today, we still love a good underdog story, and what are underdogs but those stubborn and headstrong troublemakers who simply refuse to conform?

Nearly four centuries after *Paradise Lost's* publication, many writers and artists still draw on Milton's interpretation of the Devil for inspiration. And while you will still see occasional echoes of Satan's earlier conceptualization as beastlike, grotesque, and monstrous, far more often he is portrayed as stylish, cunning, charismatic, attractive, and even a little sympathetic. Look at the charming Peter Cook in the original version of *Bedazzled*, or the beguiling Elizabeth Hurley in its remake, or the "man of wealth and taste" sung about by the Rolling Stones. We as a culture appear to have a certain bad boy fascination with Lucifer, the same we feel for anyone who refuses to follow the rules, even as society's authority figures insist that following his example is a sin of the highest order.

Chapter 3

Childhood's End

Arthur C. Clarke's science fiction novel *Childhood's End* offers an interesting take on this "nonconformist as devil" narrative. If you haven't read it, you might want to skip this bit, because I'm about to spoil the ending. In short, a race of alien beings come to Earth to usher mankind into the next phase of existence. The change is ultimately positive and necessary, but like most changes, extremely traumatic. Throughout the book, the aliens refuse to let any humans see what they look like, and in the end it's revealed why. They look like devils, complete with everything from barbed tails to bat wings. The story goes that their first intervention in human history, many thousands of years earlier, was so traumatic that we as a species immortalized their image in our conception of evil itself. We draw devils as winged and tailed because the beings who shunted us out of our cradles and into the harsh reality of life as we know it looked like that. The change was necessary for maturity, but we couldn't help but resent anything that disrupted a complacent and uncomplicated existence. What Clarke has tapped into with this book is the excellent observation that disrupters are never welcome in society, even when that disruption is ultimately for the good.

The Devil's Playthings

One of the most large-scale disruptions that a society can experience is the process of technological change. Technology has the power to make life easier, improve the standard of living, even extend health and life itself in ways once thought impossible. Change also requires us to adapt, and while humans are famously good at adaptation—it's what's enables us to flourish as a species despite our inferior size, strength, and speed—we don't really like having to do it. Change is hard, change is painful, and for that reason, change is often feared. For while it is true that technology, on average, makes people's lives better, this is not necessarily the case for all people all of the time. We are all familiar with the tragic stories of workers who have seen their livelihoods destroyed by advances in technology that render their skills, so long and dearly acquired, obsolete. Today, we read with quaint curiosity of bygone professions that seem almost absurd in light of our modern conveniences. Herman Melville's classic story *Bartleby, The Scrivener* concerns a law office that employs no less than three clerks whose entire profession is to make copies of legal documents by hand. What a waste of labor it seems, in light of the photocopiers, scanners, and printers that are fixtures in every modern office. And yet, that labor was important to the people who earned their living from it, and who had to find another line of work when their services were rendered redundant by technology. Of course, retraining is possible and necessary, but like Bartleby in the story, most of us would simply prefer not to.

The economist Joseph Schumpeter referred to this process as "creative destruction". The creation of a new technology, whether it be a labor-saving machine like the photocopier or simply a new technique for doing something more efficiently, renders older methods obsolete, and therefore destroys the demand for those methods and drives the people practicing them out of work. Like many economic concepts, this leads to much confusion among laypersons. While it's easy, and indeed appropriate, to feel sorry for displaced workers and to attempt to alleviate their suffering, it's much harder for individuals, particular those who are personally affected, to see the broader gains for society in the process of creative destruction. French economist Frederic Bastiat pointed out this problem in a famous essay entitled *That Which Is Seen and That Which Is Unseen*. We see the worker who loses his job, and lament his plight, but it's much harder to directly observe that the savings resulting from more efficient technology is ultimately capable of employing more people, and raising the overall standard of living in society.

This is the reason why history is littered with reactionary movements in opposition to new technologies. The word *saboteur* comes from a protest led by factory workers against new machines that threatened their jobs. The protesters would hurl their shoes, called sabots, into the machinery, breaking it in a futile effort to preserve their disappearing employment. The word *luddite* comes from a movement of textile workers, led by a man called Ned Ludd, who sought to prevent the use of automated weaving machines so as to protect the employment of laborers whose only marketable skills were to weave by hand.

Time has not lessened the anxieties of workers who fear displacement by technology. The American automobile industry, long in decline as foreign competitors produce superior products at lower prices, routinely receives bailouts from the federal government in the form of direct subsidies or tariffs on foreign cars. When the ridesharing service Uber began to revolutionize the way people get from point A to point B, taxi drivers around the world lobbied to ban the company from operating, or else impose regulations that would make it unprofitable. Airbnb offered a similar model for temporary lodging, and was met with the same sort of resistance from the established hotel industry. Automation in general continues to encounter broad resistance from those who fear mass unemployment and civil unrest. When it is pointed out that every technological change up to this point has resulted in a net benefit for humanity, the naysayers insist that this time it will be different, and that there is something unprecedented in the future that lies just around the corner.

Maybe they're right, but there's little reason to believe that pure stubbornness is going to do much to help. Laws that prevent new technologies from operating or regulations that impose huge compliance costs will admittedly protect the jobs of some workers, but they do so at the expense of customers who are denied a cheaper, better, and more efficient product. Moreover, history shows that efforts to suppress technological change are essentially futile. If a better way of doing something exists, eventually you won't be able to stop people from using it. Our compassion for displaced workers would be more profitably directed in helping them transition into new careers rather than clinging to a past that is simply not going to last forever.

There are, of course, plenty of other mundane, logical reasons why a person might resist innovation. Apart from the fear of losing one's job, the most obvious of these is the threat of competition. An innovation in technology risks giving competitors an advantage over established incumbents, which tend to be larger, less nimble companies with less ability to adapt to changing conditions. Often, it's easier to employ lobbyists and marketers to try to poison the new idea in the minds of the public, or else get it banned or heavily regulated by the government. For example, when a handful of black-market vaping products resulted in some heavily publicized deaths, tobacco companies were keen to represent all forms of e-cigarettes as potentially dangerous, and governments quickly responded by banning certain products from the shelves, the reasons for such tactics are obvious: vaping represents an alternative to traditional tobacco products that threatens to reduce sales of cigarettes. The people who manufacture and sell those cigarettes have a strong incentive to protect their revenues by resisting the innovation, even if it may be good for the public at large.

There are also political reasons why people in power might be hostile to new ideas. In his book, *How Innovation Works,*

Matt Ridley tells the story of coffee's introduction to Europe. A product of the new world with a bold taste and energy-boosting caffeine, it's natural that coffee was an immediate hit, but plenty of people felt threatened by the new beverage. Among them was King Charles II of England, who banned the establishment of coffee houses in 1675. It might seem a strange and trivial thing for a monarch to focus on, but it makes sense for someone whose reign is not going particularly well and who needs to keep a close watch on any signs of dissent. In Charles' official proclamation, he is surprisingly candid about his motives, while also throwing in a few token "for your own good" type arguments as well.

Whereas it is most apparent, that the Multitude of Coffee-Houses of late years set up and kept within the Kingdom, the Dominion of Wales, and the Town of Berwick on Tweed, and the great resort of Idle and disaffected persons to them, have produced very evil and dangerous effects; as well for that many Tradesmen and others, do therein mis-spend much of their time, which might and probably would otherwise by imployed in and about their Lawful Callings and Affairs; but also, for that in such houses, and by occasion of the meetings of such persons therein, diverse False, Malitious and Scandalous Reports are devised and spread abroad, to the Defamation of His Majesties Government, and to the Disturbance of the Peace and Quiet of the Realm; his Majesty hath thought it fit and necessary, That the said Coffee-houses be (for the future) put down and supressed.

In other words, the King didn't want his subjects sitting around, all caffeinated up, debating the merits of his questionable administration. After all, that's how revolutions start. Despite happening three and a half centuries ago, this incident is remarkably similar to the attitudes of modern governments towards platforms that enable free and open conversation among the citizenry. China is notorious for its hostility to the internet, utilizing the "Great Firewall of China" to limit the Chinese people's access to information and opinions not approved by the country's leadership. Nor are western democracies immune from this way of thinking. During the 2016 presidential election, then-candidate Donald Trump made headlines for suggesting that the government should have the power to "close up" the internet. Here's his full remark:

We're losing a lot of people because of the internet," Trump said. "We have to see Bill Gates and a lot of different people that really understand what's happening. We have to talk to them about, maybe in certain areas, closing that internet up in some ways. Somebody will say, 'Oh freedom of speech, freedom of speech.' These are foolish people.[5]

It's understandable that loss of money, employment, or political power might motivate a resistance to innovation, but limiting our analysis to these surface-level concerns misses something, I think, about human psychology, something more primal. It's what Arthur C. Clarke understood when he represented the agents of cataclysmic change as literal devils. There is something inherent in people that converts rational concerns into deep-seated, irrational fears that affect us in ways we sometimes can't even articulate.

John Holt, an educator who spent most of his career arguing that we should celebrate diversity and ability in children rather than compel them to conform to the arbitrary mold imposed by institutional schooling, has noticed this in the way that adults interact with the very young. Writing about the capabilities of children in his book *Escape from Childhood*, Holt observes the natural tendency of adults to recoil in horror, or at the very least disapproval, at the child who displays an uncommon level of ability.

When we read about what we call the precocity of some children of earlier times, we are skeptical, often deeply threatened. The very words "precocity" and "precocious" sound like the names of diseases. They betray our feelings that most children could not possibly have done such things and that a child who could and did must have been something of a freak. Many are so used to a sentimental and condescending view of children that when they hear of a child of four speaking Latin and Greek they feel a kind of horror. Yet there is nothing remarkable about this, even now.[6]

Bright children, those who don't behave as they're "supposed" to, represent some kind of psychic threat to adults in a way that is initially difficult to understand. While we should celebrate and encourage competence in the young (children are our future, remember) we quite often do the opposite. The question is, why? Perhaps it has something to do with jealousy. We recall our own childhoods, complete with our own unremarkable abilities and outright ineptitudes, and we find it unfair that someone else should be so far "ahead" of us. Part of this is the natural human tendency to be jealous of those who we perceive as better than ourselves, who have what we wish to have but cannot, who do what we wish to do, but are unable. More important to understanding this, however, is the similar but distinct emotion of envy.

Jealousy and envy are generally used as synonyms in casual speech, but there is an important difference. Whereas jealousy involves wanting the same things that others have for ourselves, envy is simple resentment of success, and the desire to tear down or hold back those who are liable to excel. When I was studying Russian in college, my professors liked to tell a joke poking fun at the Slavic temperament. Two Russian farmers are toiling in poverty side by side. The only difference in their circumstances is that one neighbor owns a cow which provides his family with milk, while the other has none. One day, a genie appears and offers the farmer with no livestock one wish of his choice. Faced with the endless possibilities of such an opportunity, the farmer barely hesitates. "Kill my neighbor's cow," he says.

It's a bit unfair to the Russians that they should be the butt of this joke; in fact, it applies equally to just about everyone. Faced with the choice of improving our own lot in life, or bringing others down to our level, an awful lot of people would, in spite of its perversity, quite happily choose the latter.

While the Judeo-Christian tradition holds that Pride is the deadliest of all sins, responsible for Lucifer's fall from grace and Adam and Eve's expulsion from paradise, envy, in practical terms, has been far more poisonous to human civilization. Sociologist Helmut Schoeck has written a detailed and extremely enlightening treatise, going into this subject in tremendous depth. His book, simply called *Envy*, should be required reading for anyone who wants to obtain a better understanding of human psychology and the root causes behind any number of historical events.

In the opening chapter of his book, Schoeck writes:

Envy is a drive which lies at the core of man's life as a social being, and which occurs as soon as two individuals become capable of mutual comparison. The urge to compare oneself invidiously with others can be found in some animals but with man it has acquired a special significance. Man is an envious being who, were it not for the social conventions aroused within the object of his envy, would have been incapable of developing the social systems to which we all belong today. If we were not constantly obliged to take account of other men's envy of the extra pleasure that accrues to us as we begin to deviate from a social norm, "social control" could not function.[7]

Schoeck notes that envy has generally been recognized for the corrosive influence that it is, even by the most primitive societies. Many a proverb warns against the dangers of envy, and certain social norms have arisen with the express object of avoiding the envy of others and mitigating its effects on society. Cultural taboos against boasting, talking too openly about one's finances, or accepting gifts too eagerly or without reciprocation are rooted in the idea of avoiding envy. Nevertheless, envy remains an inescapable part of the human condition. The German word *Schadenfreude*, meaning the pleasure of witnessing someone else's misfortune, reveals with uncommon candor the extent to which this perverse emotion is a fact of life.

Who is likely to be the object of envy? Generally, it is the person who stands out from the crowd, who succeeds where others fail, who refuses to conform to the level of wealth, happiness, or general prosperity that is the norm in a given society. The person who seems gifted with uncanny good fortune best watch his back, lest he arouse the resentment of his neighbors. The office worker who is promoted to a level above that of his peers may enjoy his victory only at the cost of his coworkers' friendship. The school child who aces an exam that stumped the rest of the class can look forward to the remainder of a term filled with isolation, if he is lucky, and bullying, if he is not. Scientists and inventors may get away with practicing their professions, provided that they confine their innovations to the modest and incremental. Anything too revolutionary is likely to be condemned out of hand.

We will have much more to say about the persecution of accused witches and sorcerers in a future chapter, but it is worth pausing here to note envy's role in this phenomenon. Schoeck describes the relationship between ordinary people and supposed witches as a two-way street of mutual envy, resulting in hostility that soon boils over into a desire to inflict bodily harm on the offending party.

In Europe, as elsewhere, "witch" originally meant something like "vagrant," a threatening, ill-intentioned person. The connection with the evil eye, the eye of the envious man, appears early. From time immemorial suspicion of witchcraft or black magic has fallen upon those who have had cause to be envious—of someone less ugly than themselves, of lucky parents, or the peasant with a good harvest and healthy cattle, etc. After all, bad luck can befall only those who have something to lose: good health, beauty, possessions, family. In the attempt to come to terms emotionally with the problem of misfortune, it seemed reasonable to look around for people who might be envious.

During the witch trials in Europe the accused were precisely those persons who had somehow aroused the suspicion that they were envious and hence desirous of harming others. Gradually, however, the envious man himself became the accuser, the accused being people who were good-looking, virtuous, proud and rich, or the wives of wealthy citizens. This double role played by envy in witchcraft is again apparent among primitive peoples. The outsider, the cripple, anyone at all handicapped, is suspected and regarded as responsible for damage. Yet the same primitive man is capable of asserting that another member of his tribe is only rich, powerful, a good dancer or hunter because he has gained by black magic something that should have belonged to his fellow tribesmen.[8]

We will return to the subject of witchcraft shortly, but the important point here is the way in which deviation from the norm, both in the positive or negative direction, can inspire resentment and fear, and lead to the suspicion that some unholy, supernatural power is at work. And once someone, whether possessing a hideous deformity or an uncommonly brilliant mind, is believed to be allied with the Devil, persecution is never far behind.

Scientists on Trial

If technology, innovation, and new ideas represent an existential threat in the minds of many people, how wicked, then, must seem the individuals who are responsible for creating and distributing these things? Is it any wonder that great thinkers with ideas well ahead of their times have been the subject of demonization for as long as we can remember?

In *The Fountainhead*, Ayn Rand's classic novel of individualism and artistic integrity, protagonist Howard Roark distills the essence of popular resistance to men of genius:

> *Throughout the centuries, there were men who took first steps down new roads armed with nothing but their own vision. Their goals differed, but they all had this in common: that the step was first, the road new, the vision unborrowed, and the response they received — hatred. The great creators — the thinkers, the artists, the scientists, the inventors — stood alone against the men of their time. Every great new thought was opposed. Every great new invention was denounced. But the men of unborrowed vision went ahead. They fought, they suffered and they paid. But they won.*[9]

Perhaps they did win, but it was a victory for which they certainly paid a heavy price. Indeed, even Socrates, one of the first great thinkers recorded by history, ultimately paid for his inquisitive nature with death. Plato, Socrates' student, tells the story over the course of several dialogues. Socrates has run afoul of the Athenian government and has been charged as a criminal, a charge which ultimately results in his execution by the forced drinking of hemlock. In Plato's dialogue entitled *Apology*, Socrates sums up the affidavit against him as follows:

> *It says that Socrates is a doer of evil, who corrupts the youth; and who does not believe in the gods of the state, but has other new divinities of his own.*[10]

Socrates proceeds to mount an eloquent defense against his

accusers, but alas, to no avail. While the only thing Socrates was really guilty of was being a pest who asked too many questions, succeeding in making powerful people look stupid, it is notable that the state finds it necessary to characterize him as a corrupting influence motivated by false gods or, as the original Greek would have it, *daimons*. Even in polytheistic, philosophical Athens, the charge of supernatural impiety was evidently useful in disposing of troublemakers.

There is some debate among scholars as to whether the events narrated by Plato actually happened, or whether they were merely stories told for didactic purposes to his students. Some doubt whether Socrates even existed as an actual person, rather than a mere fictional avatar for Plato's thoughts. Regardless of what the truth may be, it's clear that the dangers of nonconformity were well understood even in the comparatively civilized Athenian culture of more than two millennia ago.

In discussing scientists accused of heresy, it would be remiss not to mention Charles Darwin. Today credited with the theory of evolution, Darwin was actually one link in a long chain of theorists who gradually developed an understanding of natural selection over time. Nor was Darwin the radical iconoclast he is sometimes portrayed as today. He was himself a religious man, and expressed deeply conflicted views over the implications of his theories. He often argued with his own wife, who feared for his salvation as a result of his publications.

Darwin was not as roundly rejected by the Church as one might expect. Although some Catholic theologians did condemn his theories as heretical, the reaction was far from universal, and others accepted his views as consistent with divine creation. The Protestant Church of England was overall more hostile to Darwin than the Catholics were, as we can see in the continued rejection of evolutionary theory by some branches of Protestantism today. Still, Darwin suffered no real persecution for his views and remained active in the religious communities for the remainder of his life. In 2008, the Church of England issued a posthumous apology to Darwin for an overly emotional and vitriolic reaction to his work. Today, some fundamentalists still regard Darwin's theories as lies sown by the Devil, but on the whole, he got off pretty easy considering the far-reaching impact of his discoveries.

Perhaps the most famous example of a scientist being accused of diabolical collusion was the Italian astronomer, physicist and natural philosopher Galileo Galilei. Galileo was a major contributor to the advancement of science during the Italian Renaissance, famously demonstrating that objects of different mass fall at the same rate by dropping things off the Tower of Pisa. But it was his continuation of the work of Copernicus that got him into hot water with the Church. Throughout his life, Galileo showed no overt hostility to the Church, and was by all accounts a good Catholic. He just didn't want to let dogma get in the way of scientific truth. When he discovered through a series of observations with a telescope that the Earth revolves around the Sun, rather than standing immobile at the center of the universe as was previously thought, he ignited controversy throughout the religious and scientific world.

Some, like rival astronomer Tycho Brahe, objected to Galileo's theories on scientific grounds. The ensuing robust debate is the sort of thing that drives science forward, and posed no real problems for Galileo. It was only when the Inquisition got involved that he ran into trouble. It was argued that the heliocentric theory contradicted scripture, which spoke of the Sun rising and setting in relation to the Earth. Galileo countered that the Bible was a source for moral and spiritual truth, but was not intended to convey the specifics of scientific fact. These arguments went on for some time, but ultimately Galileo's inability to play politics with the Vatican caught up to him. He was threatened with torture if he refused to denounce his theories, and when he tried to demonstrate his findings to

Church officials, they refused to look through his telescope, which they considered to be an instrument of the Devil.

Galileo managed to avoid torture, but he was sentenced to house arrest for much of the remainder of his life and ordered to study scripture every day. No one knows for sure, but it has been said that, while delivering his public retraction before the court, Galileo muttered a last line of protest under his breath, saying "but it does move" after declaring the Earth to be a stationary body.

The Philosophers Stoned

Galileo's views may have been that of a nonconformist, but as a scientist he was comparatively respectable, given many honors and exalted positions before his ultimate downfall. But there was another class of natural philosophers obsessed with secrecy and mysticism, as well as the pursuit of goals that threatened both our understanding of the natural world and the economics of Medieval Europe. I'm speaking, of course, of the alchemists.

Perhaps it has something to do with the fact that the *al-* prefix indicates that the word comes from Arabic, the language of the heretical Saracens. Perhaps it's all the strange-looking equipment sequestered away in arcane laboratories. Perhaps it's the elaborate use of symbols and codes designed to protect professional secrets. Maybe it's simply the fact that alchemists spent a lot of time in the company of dangerous poisons and hazardous fumes. There is something about alchemy that just *seems* demonic.

What even is alchemy? In modern popular culture, this exceedingly complex field of study has been reduced to an obsessive lust for gold and the delusion that it can be created from base metals like lead. In fact, alchemy as practiced in the years leading up to the renaissance was a lot more involved, and considerably more mysterious than this contemporary caricature would lead us to believe. Lest the modern reader regard alchemy as a fringe pursuit practiced only by fanatics and weirdos, it's worth noting that no less a scientist than Isaac Newton displayed a fascination with the subject, and devoted much energy to it during his lifetime.

Most scholars now hold that alchemists were simply primitive chemists, and to a large extent this is probably true. Those with the means and the curiosity started playing around with heating metals and chemicals in order to produce a variety of reactions. The ultimate goal of alchemy was commonly known as "The Great Work", and this frequently involved the creation of something known as "The Philosopher's Stone." It is also true that an awful lot of alchemical texts talk about transmuting lesser metals into gold, as well as the creation of an elixir of eternal life. This, unfortunately, is where things get very confusing.

Alchemists tended to write down their ideas using an incredibly obscure combination of symbols and metaphors, making retrospective analysis of their texts quite difficult. In fact, we still don't really know to what extent these writings are to be taken literally. Salt, we are told, does not mean common sodium chloride, but some kind of ideal, archetypical salt. The same goes for quicksilver, sulfur, and the other substances commonly called for in alchemical experiments. The extreme difficulty in figuring out what the heck these guys are even talking about makes any attempt to replicate these experiments an exercise in futility.

In light of this, some have argued that the desire to turn lead into gold was a real one, and that descriptions of success in this endeavor may have referred to a process similar to electroplating. Others argue that the instructions for elaborate chemical processes are actually spiritual metaphors. Turning lead to gold has nothing to do with actual, physical metals. It's a metaphor for polishing up one's soul, taking something that was once dull and worthless and making it sparkle. Similarly, the reference to an elixir of life indicates not bodily immortality, but spiritual immortality. After all, the Bible speaks frequently of granting men the gift of eternal life, and nobody expects that to be taken literally. It is understood that the soul is what lives on, not the body, provided it is treated with sufficient care.

To make things even more complicated, there is a third theory that might help explain the obscurity of alchemical texts. Although a minority view, some people have hypothesized that these writings were actually sex manuals, written in code to throw puritanical authorities off the scent. There's a lot of talk of inserting or submerging one substance into another, descriptions of fiery pyrotechnics that are not dissimilar from the types of visual metaphors you see in romantic comedies when the lead couple kiss for the first time. The various fluids under discussion have obvious analogues, and the description of eternal life could easily refer to reproduction, or to put it another way, genetic immortality. Given the taboos around openly discussing sexual matters at the time, it would make sense that such writing would be in code, but at the same time it's hard to extend such an interpretation to the vast body of alchemical literature. In any case, the metaphor would have to be stretched so thin as to be completely incomprehensible, thus defeating the purpose of writing such a manual in the first place.

My own view is that all three of these interpretations are correct to a greater or lesser extent. Some alchemists were writing about chemistry, some were writing about spirituality, and some were writing about gettin' it on. The fact that we don't know which is which only adds to the difficulties in interpretation.

Alchemists as a whole were not regarded as heretics by the Church or executed for their views. Indeed, such respected theologians as Thomas Aquinas and Albertus Magnus devoted considerable study to the field. Like other scientists, however, alchemists sometimes ran into trouble with the law. King Henry

IV of England banned the practice of alchemy early in the fifteenth century, fearing that the ability to create gold out of lesser metal would threaten the wealth of the monarchy. While this ban was eventually lifted, a few incautious practitioners nevertheless paid a price for their nonconformist field of study.

Alexander Seton was one such man. A seventeenth century Scottish alchemist, Seton was born into a respectable family, but quickly fell into disrepute when he began what appeared to be a series of successful demonstrations of his power to transmute lead into gold. After a European tour showcasing his findings, Seton was summoned by Christian II, Elector of Saxony, to demonstrate his findings. Unable to appear at once, Seton sent a representative in his place who, through the use of a mysterious red powder of Seton's invention, appeared to successfully produce gold to the satisfaction of Christian and his court. The rest of the story does not go so well for Seton, however.

> Christian again invited Seton to the court and this time there could be no refusal. At first, the Elector appeared to be friendly, but it soon became clear that he would not be satisfied with demonstrations of transmutation: he demanded the secret of the powder. The Cosmopolite as steadfast in his refusal to part with it, so when sweet reasonableness failed, Christian had recourse to sterner measures. Seton was put on the rack, scourged, pierced with pointed irons, and burned with molten lead; but all in vain. He would reveal nothing. Christian would doubtless have continued the torture still further, but Seton was now at death's door, and were he to die the last chance of wresting the secret from him would be lost. He was therefore put in solitary confinement in a gloomy dungeon constantly guarded by relays of soldiers.[11]

Eventually, Seton was able to escape with the help of some influential friends, but the tortures he had suffered ultimately proved too much for him, and he died within a year later.

Marco Bragadino was another alchemist whose career followed a similar path to Seton's. After achieving some success, he found his boasts were unequal to his abilities. He fled his home city of Venice when rumors began to spread both about his dishonesty and the unholy nature of his powers. The two black dogs he kept as pets were said to bewitched, and he was forced to move on to Bavaria, where his brief alliance with Duke William V turned sour when he was unable to produce gold in the quantities demanded. Bragadino was summarily executed by beheading, and his unfortunate dogs were also killed.

It can be debated to what extent fear of the supernatural contributed to the deaths of Seton, Bragadino, and others. No doubt, part of their infamy resulted from their willingness to lie and use trickery to prop up their own reputations. Con men, after all, cannot be expected to last long in an environment where angering the aristocracy was liable to result in death. Indeed, it would be wrong to say that the Catholic Church has displayed a systematic hostility to science in general over the years. The above examples notwithstanding, it should be pointed out that the Church has played a big role in sponsoring universities, inventors, philosophers, and scientists since the Medieval period. It is only when discoveries come into conflict with or threaten established dogmas that there has been any real tension between science and religion. For example, the Church's historical opposition to weapon technologies and birth control practices stem not from an inherent distaste for discovery, but from a principled standpoint of Catholic morality. I would hate for my words to be interpreted as an unqualified attack on any specific denomination, or indeed on religion itself. I merely wish to point out those instances in which a refusal to conform to majority views have been represented as demonic or diabolic.

The stories presented in this chapter are intended to be illustrative of a general hostility and fear, not of science itself, but surrounding the use of techniques regarded as occult or supernatural, serving as an important bridge between the scientists put on trial for their discoveries, and the similarly persecuted figures of religion and mysticism discussed in the following chapters.

Chapter 4

Saints And Martyrs

Contrary to my initial intentions, my research for this book has led me to come down fairly hard on the Catholic Church and the Christian faith in general. I have no desire to condemn anyone's faith or malign the way in which they worship. My goal is merely to defend individualism and nonconformity from accusations of diabolism and wickedness in general. My inadvertent commentary on the church is the result of two factors: first, that the church has been the dominant source of established authority in Western civilization for much of the last two thousand years, and second, that it is pretty much only Christians who actually believe in the Devil or in demons in general. So, while you may find atheistic regimes such as the Soviet Socialists in Russia that are extremely hostile to nonconformists, you will not find them employing the tactics of demonization in the literal sense in which I am interested. Likewise, while there are some pagan religions that embrace a belief in demons, people who hold these beliefs seldom hold the positions of societal power necessary to engage in any systematic persecution.

The result of all this is that, while I have no particular axe to grind against Christianity, the historical facts of the Inquisition, witch trials, and hostility towards certain scientists tend to reflect rather badly on the Church. There was a time, however, when embracing the teachings of Christ was itself an act of nonconformity, and there has certainly been no shortage of believers who have faced persecution for their convictions. In many ways, the history of the world is the history of religious persecution, as dominant faiths attempt to eradicate alternative belief systems or splinter groups that threaten the stability of orthodoxy. In the interest of balance, therefore, and to clarify that the point of this book is not to attack Christians but to defend free thinkers, let us delve into some examples of pious souls who were demonized for their trouble.

The Bible itself warns that religious persecution is to be the inevitable fate of the believer. The Second Letter of Timothy makes this very clear, stating: "Indeed all who desire to lead a godly life in Christ Jesus will be persecuted."[12] The First Letter of John concurs, saying: "Do not wonder, brethren, that the world hates you."[13] Jesus himself, in his Sermon on the Mount, even offers solace to those he knows will suffer for their faith: "Blessed are those who are persecuted for righteousness' sake, for theirs is the kingdom of heaven."[14] It is clear from these passages that the early Christians were intimately familiar with the dangers of having new ideas that contradicted established doctrine.

The Bible's warnings were not idle ones, for the life of an early Christian was a risky one. After the Roman Emperor Nero began executing Christians in a display of his typical cruelty, Christianity was made an official crime punishable by death, and the systematic persecution of Christians began to spread throughout the empire. This was for political as much as religious reasons. While the laws did insist that Roman deities continue to be honored and worshipped alongside the Emperor, Christianity's emphasis on being loyal to a Messiah or monotheistic God was seen as a threat to the Emperor's authority. Christians were thus forced to choose whether they would be loyal to the Emperor, or to Christ, and those who chose the latter were killed.

The Romans were not the only ones who took issue with Christianity. Many Jewish people regarded the religion as idolatrous and full of strange practices which, garbled and misunderstood, appeared to be demonic and wicked. For example, one common rumor held that Christians ate the flesh of murdered babies. This was nothing more than a failure to understand the symbolism of the communion rite. When Christians spoke of drinking the blood of Christ and eating his body, the uninitiated assumed that they were eating actual babies. Another source of the confusion was the habit of Christians to refer to each other as "brother" or "sister". Upon hearing married couples use these terms, the local Jews were horrified, assuming that God's commandment against incest was being violated. Stories such as these contributed to the demonization and persecution of early Christians, even before the sectarian infighting began.

Modern Christianity is home to many denominations, each with its own different canonical literature and different interpretations of scripture. This is nothing, however, compared to the confused tapestry of sectarian beliefs that sprung up in the first couple of centuries after the death of Christ. Many of these can be lumped together under the umbrella term of Gnosticism, a cluster of Christian denominations characterized by a belief in revealed divine *gnosis* (the Greek word for knowledge) which could be received by the faithful in order to make sense of the universe. While early Catholicism developed the idea of the Holy Trinity and stressed the need to reach God through his emissary on Earth, the Pope, many of the gnostic sects focused on reconciling the radically different temperaments of God as portrayed in the Old and New Testaments. The Old Testament God is jealous, wrathful, and frequently cruel. The New Testament God is loving, merciful, and pacifistic. The Gnostics theorized that this could only be explained by a universal dualism, a cosmic balance between good and evil, where neither side was given a permanent upper hand. Thus was born the idea of the demiurge, a blind idiot creator deity who beset mankind with plagues and floods and poison monkeys, while the true God ruled above in the ineffable spirit of loving kindness, as depicted in the New Testament.

That these two coequal deities were at constant war with one another gave the Gnostics an explanation for the existence of evil in the world, a continually thorny problem for those theologians that hold that God is both all-powerful, all-benevolent, and interested in the fate of his creations. One of the most prominent exponents of this dualistic view of the universe was a teacher called Mani, whose huge following included Saint Augustine before he converted to Catholicism, as detailed in his famous *Confessions*.

Of course, to the Catholics, Manicheanism was regarded as a terrible heresy. The idea that God must contend with an evil force just as great as himself flew in the face of the essential doctrine of God's omnipotence, and while the deity could be conceived of as having a three-fold nature, Christianity was still very much a monotheistic religion. The introduction of the Demiurge was a degradation into the pagan polytheism the Church had opposed from the beginning, and therefore could not be tolerated. Moreover, the various Gnostic sects, including not only Manicheanism but also Valentinian and Sethian branches, tended disturbingly towards obscure mysticism, with talk of astral light, the mysterious Abraxas, and blazing stars. The Gnostic Gospel of Thomas is a deeply metaphorical and symbolic text, firmly rejected from the official canons of Catholicism, Protestantism, and the Orthodox Church. All this mystical mumbo jumbo was reminiscent of Simon Magus, and other heretics who dabbled in magic and the occult in defiance of God's commandment "thou shalt not suffer a witch to live."

As a universalist proselytizing religion, Christianity, depended on conversion and attracting new followers for its survival. Such a fragmentary network of fundamentally opposed belief systems was therefore bad for business, and over the next few centuries, the Catholic Church worked tirelessly to destroy these heretical offshoots and bring the faithful in line with a single, unified theology. There was simply no room for nonconformists if the religion of Christ was going to survive.

To the Catholics' credit, this strategy worked. The Gnostics who survived disappeared underground, forced to practice their minority beliefs in secret for hundreds of years. Occasionally, however, a new branch would gain enough popularity to emerge and represent a threat to the Church. In the thirteenth century, a group of Gnostics known as the Cathars became prominent in France. The Cathars shared the essentially Gnostic view of the wickedness and degradation of the material world, and sought escape to a blessed realm of divine light. They permitted female priests and were somewhat more casual about sexual matters than mainstream Christians. In 1209, the Pope declared war on the Cathars and they were subsequently wiped out in a bloody conflict that decimated the French population.

In the fifteenth century, the Adamite movement spring up in central Europe. Adamites believed themselves to be so spiritually pure that none of their deeds could be considered sinful, with the predictable consequence of a lot of orgies. Here again, believers were put on trial for heresy and burned at the stake as punishment for refusing to conform to the teachings of Catholicism.

In Spain, a Catholic woman named Maria de Santo Domingo began teaching a theology that had much in common with Buddhist meditation, stressing the holy value of emptying the mind of conscious thought to achieve enlightenment. Her followers, who called themselves the Alumbrados, were mostly killed by the Inquisition for their radical views.

A sixteenth century German religious society, non-threateningly named The Family of Love, taught that the Bible was not to be taken literally, but was rather an allegorical statement of God's relation to man. In an uncommon display of leniency, members of this group were mostly only imprisoned and exiled rather than outright murdered.

All of these groups represent the dangers of daring to think differently, and the commonplace nature of martyrdom among religious nonconformists. Seemingly harmless ideas such as that women can be priests, that there are many paths to god, and that maybe sex isn't inherently evil, were demonized as unholy products of Satan's trickery, and punished in the severest possible terms.

The Knights Templar

Much of the symbolism, fear, and anxiety we now associate with secret societies, black magic, and even Satanism owe their origins to the Knights Templar, a military order of crusading, Catholic knights established in the twelfth century. According to Eliphas Levi, their stated purpose was "to protect Christians on pilgrimage to the holy places." It would be difficult, however, to find an organization whose reputation crashed and burned so dramatically over the course of its existence. The Knights Templar went from being perceived as holy warriors operating in the name of God, to monstrous idolaters and cultists who participated in the most obscene and barbaric rituals imaginable.

There are various reasons for this. Stationed as they were in the far eastern reaches of the Holy Roman Empire, the Templars were somewhat isolated from their Christian brethren. As military men under constant threat of attack, they were understandably rather paranoid, and this paranoia manifested itself in a doctrine of extreme secrecy surrounding the rites and rituals of the order. These were undoubtedly influenced by the local philosophies of the Middle East, including the Jewish Kabbalah, pagan polytheism, Egyptian mythology, as well as the tenets of Islam, Buddhism, and Hinduism. The third piece of the puzzle was that, as successful crusaders, the Templars managed to acquire through pillage a great deal of wealth. Soon, they expanded from their humble roots of just nine founding Knights into an order than stretched across the whole of Europe.

Stories of a secretive order of knights, amassing huge

quantities of riches and engaging in heathen rituals began to filter back to Rome and the rest of Europe, and the Templars developed a reputation as a group of frighteningly powerful heretics. Of particular concern was the order's alleged idolatry, the worship of a profane goat-headed god called Baphomet. Baphomet will be an at least vaguely recognizable figure to most readers: apart from his goat head, he possesses wings and a human body notable for its hermaphroditic qualities. Although modern Satanists have adopted Baphomet as a symbol, and most laypersons understand the symbol in that context, the historical use of the figure is not exactly demonic, although it is admittedly difficult to untangle the truth given the diversity of opinions on the subject.

For example, in his history of magic, Eliphas Levi, a Christian occultist, denounces the knights for their obedience to this "monstrous idol". On the other hand, as the translator of that work, occult scholar Arthur Edward Waite, points out:

> *Elsewhere Eliphas Levi says: (a) That the hypothetical idol Baphomet was a symbolical figure representing the First Matter of the* Magnum Opus, *which is the Astral Light; (b) That it signified further the god Pan, which may be identified with "the Christ of dissident sacradotalism"; (c) That the Baphometic head is "a beautiful allegory which attributes to thought alone the first and creative cause"; and finally, (d) That it is "nothing more than an innocent and even a pious hieroglyph".*[15]

Levi was the earliest and most prolific writer to address the subject of Baphomet in detail, so his opinions carry some weight, even if they blatantly contradict themselves, as they appear to do. To add to the confusion, by far the most common image of Baphomet these days is a drawing done by Levi himself for his work *The Doctrine and Ritual of Transcendental Magic*, in which he celebrates the figure rather than condemning it. It would appear that here Levi is letting his Catholicism temporarily get the better of the dispassionate scholarship he displays in his other writings.

The Knights Templar managed to survive into the fourteenth century before their excesses proved too much for either the Church or the European heads of State. Chief among their antagonists was King Philip of France, who regarded the Templars as a threat to his authority. Author and historian Thomas Keightley elaborates:

Their wealth was great; their possessions in France were most extensive; they were connected with the noblest families in the realm; they were consequently, now that they seemed to have given up all ideas of making any further efforts in the East, likely to prove a serious obstacle in the way of the establishment of the absolute power of the crown. They were finally very generally disliked on account of their excessive pride and arrogance, and it was to be expected that in an attack on their power and their privileges the popular favour would be with the king.[16]

John Michael Greer goes on to succinctly tell of the subsequent downfall of the Templars.

On Friday, October 13, 1307, royal officials across France raided Templar properties in the kingdom and arrested every Templar they could find. The charge was heresy. The captive Templars were tortured to make them confess to a laundry list of crimes. The following year, Pope Clement V ordered Templars throughout Europe arrested, and in 1312 the Knights Templar order was dissolved by the Council of Vienne.[17]

The Knights Templar remain a source of fascination within the Western Mystery tradition. Gerald Gardner, founder of the Wiccan religion, referenced them extensively in his early writings, and it's clear that the idea of a secret magical society had great appeal to him—not surprising given his earlier association with the Hermetic Order of the Golden Dawn.

To this day, nobody really knows exactly what kind of mischief the Templars got up to, and the anxiety this provoked in the rich and powerful has been echoed many times throughout history in the form of conspiracy theories against the Freemasons, the Bavarian Illuminati, and countless other groups. The Templars are notable not only for how early they arrived on the scene, and how much influence they had, but for the overt accusations of diabolism leveled against them in addition to concern over political upheaval or envy of their wealth and power.

Selected Martyrs

As we move from groups to individuals martyred for their religious beliefs, we come across several interesting characters. Of particular interest is the early Christian legend of Saint Cyprian of Antioch, illustrating that sometimes you just can't win. Cyprian lived in the fourth century CE. He went by the title of "the magician" and was said to practice sorcery and black magic. The story goes that Cyprian was approached by a customer asking for a love potion to win the affections of Justina, a pious Christian woman. Depending on who tells the legend, this section is likely to contain all manner of colorful descriptions of Cyprian conversing with demons and exhorting Satan to work his will, but the chief takeaway is that the potion had no effect on tempting the righteous young woman into sin. Cyprian was reportedly so impressed with Justina's ability to withstand evil and the power of the cross that he immediately renounced his old ways and converted to Christianity, at which point he burned all his old books on the necromantic arts.

This conversion did little to improve Cyprian's life, however, as soon thereafter both he and Justina were captured, tortured, and beheaded for the crime of being Christians and refusing to renounce their faith. This was part of the religious persecutions enacted by Roman Emperor Diocletian, who initially targeted Manicheans as an immoral and corrupting influence, before turning his attention to more orthodox Christians. Both Cyprian and Justina are now recognized as saints and martyrs in the Catholic Church.

Martyrdom was not limited to the Roman period. Giordano Bruno was a sixteenth century Dominican who was put to death for his nonconformist beliefs. Bruno is often cited in the same breath as Galileo by those eager to demonstrate the Church's hostility towards science, and it is true that, like Galileo, Bruno challenged the geocentric model of the universe that was considered to be correct at the time. However, a closer look at Bruno indicates that he is better placed in the company of religious thinkers persecuted for their beliefs than with the scientists who challenged religious orthodoxy. As Gareth Knight observes in his *A History of White Magic:*

Although Bruno has been hailed as a martyr for science, recent scholarship has revealed that he was in fact advocating a new religious system wherein the solar system was of the pattern of many other suns and systems created by God. This is close to the physical pattern of the universe revealed by modern science but Bruno's motives were principally religious. He saw man as capable of expanding his consciousness by his own efforts until he became as God.[18]

Bruno was burned at the stake for heresy in 1600.

The Maid of Orleans

Another martyr of some notoriety made the mistake of speaking too openly about her personal relationship with God. Joan of Arc was born to a poor peasant family in France, but soon into her teenage years she began reporting visions of the Archangel

Gabriel, Saint Margaret, and Saint Catherine. She believed that she was being called upon by God to help her country in the war against England, and at the age of sixteen she managed to gain an audience at the royal court. After making several astute military predictions, she was allowed by King Charles VII to travel with the troops in full military attire. She quickly proved an adept warrior and strategist, helping to secure a number of military victories for the French.

That an illiterate teenage girl born into poverty should become a military hero was one of those accidents of history that seem, in hindsight, almost unbelievably strange. Joan so excelled at everything she attempted that it was hard not to believe her claims of divine sponsorship. Her career was cut short, however, when she was captured by the English and put on trial for heresy.

Everything about the trial was unfair. The English authorities could find no real evidence against Joan, and violated ecclesiastical law in even having the trial in the first place, by refusing to allow Joan an advocate in her defense. To the astonishment of everyone present, she was able to deftly avoid theological traps laid by the prosecution designed to trick her into condemning herself. It must be remembered that Joan could not read or write, and was only nineteen years old at the time, so how she had managed to acquire such a shrewd grip on complex theology was a mystery.

Under the law at the time, a single count of heresy was not punishable by death, so the court needed to find a second charge against Joan. They got around this difficulty by accusing her of cross-dressing, since she was known to fight in men's military attire. Joan protested this on theological grounds, again showing uncanny knowledge of Christian scholarship, and agreed to wear clothing appropriate for women. But none of it mattered. At just nineteen years old she was convicted of heresy and sentenced to burn at the stake. They burned her body three times until only ashes were left, and these they threw into the Seine river determined to prevent any rumors of escape from arising among her supporters.

At the end of the Hundred Years War some twenty years later, Pope Callixtus III authorized a reexamination of Joan's alleged heresy. The Church found no evidence against her, and she was posthumously acquitted of all wrongdoing, becoming a kind of folkloric hero to the French people. In 1920, she was officially canonized as a saint by Pope Benedict XV.

More than half a millennium after her death, Joan remains a symbol of how much a single person can accomplish with sufficient determination and disregard for traditional societal limits. She also serves as a warning of what can happen to those who refuse to conform to the mores of their times.

The Unholy Fathers

One would think that if anyone would be immune from accusations of impiety, heresy, and the influence of black magic, it would be the head of the Roman Catholic Church. In fact, the Pope has been a relatively frequent target of smear campaigns that allege some kind of demonic affiliation. The reasons for this are various, and include political jockeying, jealousy, opposition to proposed reforms, and mere superstition. As God's representative on Earth, dressed in fancy robes, sequestered away in the Vatican with all manner of ancient texts, and presiding over the ritualistic ceremonies that characterize the Catholic Mass, it's only natural that the suspicion of strange and occult powers would fall on such a person. In fact, the term "hocus pocus", used to describe acts of magical mumbo jumbo, is belied to derive from a mishearing or deliberate parody of the Latin phrase "hoc est corpus", used in the Mass to mean "this is the body". Combine these with the immense power of the papacy and the envy that power would surely aspire in others, and you have a recipe for diabolic accusations.

Numerous popes have been the object of whispered rumors over the years. Leo II and Honorius III were said to have authored grimoires, the goetic magical textbooks of the Medieval period that inspired much fear among the righteous. In reality, these were probably either misattributions designed to damage the Pope's reputation, or else corruptions of common books of prayer. Indeed, an examination of actual grimoires finds that they frequently resemble lengthy prayers to God, Jesus, and the angels more than anything else, so this misunderstanding is not hard to imagine.

Other popes, such as Leo I and Gregory III, were accused of sorcery by their bishops or political rivals, who objected to the new directions in which they were taking the Church. Of particular interest among these is the case of Sylvester II.

Sylvester II was Pope for just four years, from 999 to 1003 CE. He was known as a champion of mathematics and science, and did much to bridge the divide between Islamic and Christian scholars. He also had his enemies. It's fair to say that no other Pope has attracted as much suspicion of dark magic as poor Sylvester. Rumors began to swirl about that he had made a pact with the devil in order to gain his considerable wealth and power. It was also believed that he had a demon mistress, or succubus named Meridiana who would satisfy his carnal lusts as well as helping his papacy through supernatural intervention. He was also believed to possess a bronze head, given to him by the devil, that was capable of predicting the future.

One such prophesy held that Sylvester would die in Jerusalem, and so the Pope avoided that city entirely during his reign. He failed to account, however, for the literal nature such prophesies often display, and ended up dying in a church in Rome known as The Holy Cross of Jerusalem. Legend now holds that his tomb will run with sweat in advance of the death of a prominent person, particularly if that person is another pope.

At the end of the thirteenth century, Boniface VIII faced similar allegations. Like Sylvester, he was accused of selling his soul in order to gain the papacy. People said that he conjured demons, sacrificed chickens as part of his occult rituals, and wore a ring which contained an imp which would assist in his ambitions and frustrate his enemies. When he died, it was said that the heavens opened in a huge tempest of thunder, lightning, and dragon fire to mark his passing. These rumors were fueled by the fact that the hot-tempered Boniface had a very contentious relationship with various European heads of state, who wanted nothing more than to undermine his authority as Pope.

In the sixteenth century, suspicions of devil-dealing again fell on the papacy under the reign of Sixtus V. As an archbishop, Sixtus had spent time in Spain investigating heresy charges and generally making enemies. When he became Pope, the Spanish bishops responded by leveling the usual accusations of sorcery, pacts with the devil, and grotesque ritual practices in an effort to overthrow him. An amusing story tells of a meeting between Sixtus and the Devil on the Pope's death bed, five years into his reign. Apparently, the Devil had promised Sixtus six years as pope, and Sixtus was now upset that his end was coming prematurely. The Devil responded that Sixtus had sentenced a man to execution one year before his appointed time, and as punishment he must forfeit the last year of his life. It would appear that in this case, the Devil won the argument, for Sixtus did indeed die after only five years, not six.

One might argue that it's poetic justice for the leader of the Catholic Church to fall victim to the same accusations that they leveled against the powerless during the years of the Inquisition, hoisted by their own petard, as it were. The fact is, however, that popes were never habitually subjected to the kinds of cruel tortures and executions we'll learn about in the next chapter. There is something to be said about glass houses, though. Popes who dared to buck tradition and make waves in the Church's established orthodoxy were always going to meet opposition, but by fixating on magical practices and conversing with spirits as the unholiest of sins, they opened themselves up to a more literal form of demonization.

The King of Kings

There is, of course, no more famous martyr in the history of religion than Jesus Christ himself. The teachings of Jesus were also radical beyond any that came before him. He sought to replace the sectarian tribalism of the Old Testament with a universal doctrine of divine love. Whereas Yahweh advised that an eye should be taken for an eye, and that death should be the penalty for even minor infractions, Jesus admonished his followers to love their neighbors as themselves, refrain from criticism of others, turn the other cheek against aggression, and give willingly to thieves and swindlers. He also upended the idea the of salvation by downplaying the importance of following commandments or performing good works, stressing instead that faith alone was the key to Heaven.

The coming of Jesus is presaged by a number of miraculous events. The coming of the Messiah is foretold in prophesy and visions by several Old Testament writers, most notably Ezekiel. When Jesus is born, the three Magi from the East are drawn to him by a star which appears in the sky. Apocryphal gospels concerning Jesus' youth demonstrate him performing miraculous feats that would be condemned as sorcery if performed by anyone else, such as bringing clay pigeons to life and defeating dragons. Of course, the more orthodox miracles of the adult Jesus, walking on water, turning water into wine, et cetera, are well known.

Unsurprisingly, there were those who did regard these feats of magical dexterity as unholy abominations. Jews who were unconvinced that Christ fit the description of their prophesied Messiah suspected Jesus as a phony and an imposter. They also feared that Jesus' leadership was degrading divine worship from something immaterial and innately spiritual to a degraded and coarse cult of personality. In his book *Magic: A History of Its Rites and Rituals,* French occultist Eliphas Levi expounds upon this point.

> *The Jews accused that faith [in Jesus] of having materialized belief and idealized earthly things.* In our Doctrine and Ritual of Transcendental Magic *we have related the scandalous parable of the* Sepher Toldos Jeshu *which was invented to support the accusation. It is related in the* Talmud *that Jesus ben Sabta, or the son of the divorced woman, having studied profane mysteries in Egypt, set up a false stone in Israel and led the people into idolatry.*[19]

Jesus was eventually put on trial before a Jewish judicial body known as the Sanhedrin, and charged with a number of crimes relating to the practice of magic, idolatry, and other practices in conflict with Jewish law. He was condemned for performing exorcisms, for claiming to be the son of God, and for violating the Commandment against working on the Sabbath. It was this trial that ultimately led to his crucifixion and death.

Religious Persecution Today
We need not think that persecution for praying to the wrong God or reading the wrong holy book went out of style with the Inquisition. Indeed, it's still going on to this day, and in greater numbers than you might imagine. In America, where freedom of religion is enshrined as a constitutional right, we hear much about the dangers of Islamophobia, fearing that innocent people might be condemned because they share a religious identity with some high-profile terrorist organization. These fears are justified, but we must also remember that in predominantly Islamic countries, Christians are not only discriminated against,

but actually killed for their beliefs.

Opinion polls conducted by Pew Research have found that the belief that apostasy, the act of leaving the Muslim faith, should be punishable by death is a mainstream view, even in moderate Muslim countries like Egypt and Indonesia. A 2019 report commissioned by Britain's Foreign Secretary found that Christians represented the most persecuted religious group in the world, and that violence against Christians in the Middle East was reaching levels approaching genocide. The World Watch List has found that roughly 3,000 Christians are killed for their faith each year.

The Pew Research Center has collected data on religious persecution around the world, and what they found is rather shocking. As of 2015, Christians faced persecution in 128 countries, Muslims in 125 countries, Jews in 74 countries, and pagan folk religions in 32 countries. Hindus, Buddhists, and even atheists were also reported as victims of persecution, although on a smaller scale. Nor do these findings only reflect the actions of hate groups and terrorist organizations. For every religion, persecution was sponsored by the government in more than half of the countries listed. Even people who belong to the majority religion of a particular place are not necessarily safe, as blasphemy is still illegal in many countries, rendering criticism even of one's own religion a dangerous enterprise.

We like to think that the practice of executing people for holding different religious views went out of style with the Middle Ages. Unfortunately, although there has been much global progress and many Western countries now explicitly protect freedom of religion, in many parts of the world it's still dangerous to be a nonconformist.

Chapter 5

Witches And Warlocks

Perhaps no group of nonconformists has suffered as much, both reputationally and in terms of actual persecution, as those whom we call witches, sorcerers, and occultists. In fact, that these classes of persons should be lumped together under one umbrella is a bit strange, for they differ immensely both in their origins, their goals, and their actual practices. What they do have in common is an interest in, and practical application of, forces which seem strange and foreign to the average layperson. The word "occult" literally means "hidden", and an occultist is therefore someone who seeks out undiscovered truths, frequently maintaining a secret knowledge tradition to assist in this aim. In modern times, the widespread availability of printed books, not to mention the internet, has rendered any claim to secrecy laughable, but still most people remain as ignorant of the subject as they do of organic chemistry, fluid dynamics, or any other field that requires specialized study.

Contrary to its depiction in popular media, there is nothing sinister about occultism as it is practiced today. Its goals are similar to the goals of various traditions of eastern mysticism practiced by some Buddhists and Hindus. In short, the aim of most occultists is to discover ways, usually through meditation and similar practices, to expand their consciousness, moving ever closer to the divine, and through this process to gain mastery over their own minds and bodies, ultimately reaching the full potential of mankind. It is not a normal pastime, to be sure, but neither is it anything to be afraid of. We don't typically demonize the bodybuilder who strives for physical perfection, and so should we avoid demonizing the occultist who strives for spiritual and mental perfection.

Distinct from the occultist is the sorcerer and alchemist. We have dealt with alchemists somewhat in Chapter 3, and need not repeat much about them here save that they essentially practiced an amalgam of primitive chemistry and symbolic metaphysics, in which terms like Sulphur, Quicksilver, and Saltpeter stood for intangible spiritual concepts. The history of alchemy is clouded with deliberate deception and indecipherable metaphor, but it is likely that The Great Work which alchemists speak of was not, as is commonly asserted, to transmute lead into gold, but to symbolically transform the "base" or common person into a rare and precious specimen of spiritual enlightenment.

Much of western occultism is also firmly rooted in the traditions of Judaism. The Kabbalah, or Qabalah as it is sometimes spelled, refers to a body of received wisdom studied by Jewish mystics. Among other things, it deals with the nature of creation and symbolic language used to convey hidden meaning in scripture. As an oral tradition, there is much dispute as to the actual age of Kabbalistic teachings, but at least since the Renaissance these have been a cornerstone of occult studies.

Much of occultism's bad reputation likely comes from sorcery, and the medieval grimoires that purported to contain spells of great power. Anyone who bothers to read these books can see that they are obvious nonsense, designed to prey upon the credulous and power hungry, and using shock value to gain notoriety. Still, even these books are not overtly demonic or Satanic, although the casual reader could be forgiven for thinking otherwise. Grimoires such as the *Greater and Lesser Keys of Solomon the King* promise the aspiring sorcerer riches and power through the evocation of demons, as catalogued by early Christian and Jewish theologians. While that may sound like pretty dodgy work, there is an important distinction to be made. The operations described have nothing to do with *worshipping* or otherwise glorifying the infernal powers. Quite to the contrary, it is always in the name of God that the demons are called forth, bound, and forced to submit to the will of the operator. The demons are not, then, treated as deities to be admired or emulated, but as slaves to the Almighty, free to carry out the sorcerer's orders only with divine permission. It is worth noting that the author of these grimoires is traditionally held to be King Solomon the Wise, a man eminently favored by God in the Old Testament. It is inconceivable that a man so renowned for his wisdom and holiness would turn to Satanism and demonolatry in his later years. The misinterpretation of Solomonic magic, as well as a tendency to take it far too seriously, is one of the things that contributed to the Church's, and by extension society at large's, negative perceptive of occultism.

As a consequence of co-mingling ideas in the late nineteenth and early twentieth centuries, modern witches, Wiccans, and neopagans tend to borrow heavily from an eclectic blend of occult traditions, but in earlier times there was hardly any overlap between them. Witches were simply wise women, herbalists, healers, sometimes even priestesses of pagan, polytheistic religions. Witches often lived alone, kept animals as pets, possessed knowledge unknown to others, and could perform feats, such as using herbs to heal a wound, that seemed mysterious. Sometimes, they might employ toxic plants such as belladonna or the red and white speckled *Anamita Muscaria* mushrooms so popular among cartoon artists to induce visions or "night flights", but more on that later. As ever, a lack of understanding and a fear of the unknown tended towards witches being demonized and ostracized rather than celebrated for their abilities.

The rise of monotheistic religions with their animosity towards competing belief systems, as well as Biblical commandments such as "thou shalt not suffer a witch to live"[20] were particularly unhelpful. Thus began a systematic effort to delegitimize the gods of old religions, and condemn any spiritual knowledge that did not come directly from the word of Yahweh.

In fact, the biblical injunctions used as justification for the persecution of witches are a bit odd, when you think about them. The main charge against witches, from a Christian point of view, is that they have made a pact with the Devil, who has given them power to do harm to mankind in exchange for their immortal souls. But as Rossell Hope Robbins helpfully points out in *The Encyclopedia of Witchcraft and Demonology*, all of the verses dealing with witchcraft come from the Old Testament, in other words, from the Jewish religion which had no real concept of the Devil or Hell to begin with. Moreover, the Hebrew words that have traditionally been translated as "witch" or "witchcraft" actually have a variety of possible meanings. For example, the Hebrew word *kaskagh* in the famous verse "Thou shalt not suffer a witch to live" actually means "poisoner" rather than "witch." It would be fairly sensible for the ancient Hebrews to prescribe strict punishment for those who would attack others with poison, far more so than this mysterious condemnation of witches, when it's unclear that the Hebrews even had such a concept.

The infamous Witch of Endor could alternately be translated as a woman who kept animal familiars (or possibly pets). Elsewhere in the Bible, acts of witchcraft or sorcery could just as easily be interpreted as prohibitions on juggling, fortune telling, and astrology. That jugglers and astrologers should meet with disapproval is not surprising (as something of a juggler myself, I can attest that even today we are not welcome in most respectable homes). It is merely a continuation of the thesis that those who display extraordinary, nonconforming, or poorly understood talents are seldom celebrated for them.

It is distressing to think that centuries of inquisition, witch trials, burnings, hangings, and unspeakable tortures should have come about due to a mistranslation. On the other hand, since witches continued to display strange behaviors that the ignorant would find threatening, it is probable that, even in the absence of explicit biblical justification, people would have found some other reason for their attacks on pagans and practitioners of old folk magic traditions.

The Horned King

Have you ever wondered why Satan looks the way he does? We all recognize the common depiction of the arch-fiend with horns, a forked tail, goat legs, cloven hooves, and a pitchfork. But where did this image come from? It certainly did not originate with Arthur C. Clarke's overlords, or even with Milton's portrayal of Lucifer in *Paradise Lost*. These authors were drawing from a much older tradition of pictorial representations of the devil. Nor is this imagery unique to Christianity. In fact, people have been conjuring up images that might look suspiciously similar to the modern vision of Satan for many thousands of years.

Students of mythology will no doubt have noticed the parallels between our pictures of the devil and the fauns and satyrs of the ancient Greeks, woodland gods or spirits that resemble a cross between a goat and a man. Most famous of these was the god Pan, who was something of a trickster deity among the Greeks, but far from the embodiment of evil. The various shenanigans he got up to were not much different from the foibles of Zeus, Ares, and the other gods of the Greek pantheon. What made Pan different was his wild, somewhat chaotic nature. He personified the wilderness itself, with all the accompanying beauty and danger. That we get the word "panic" from his name is a testament to how English-speaking people have regarded this fascinating character over the centuries.

It's also no coincidence that Pan looks an awful lot like the Devil, or indeed, that the Devil looks an awful lot like him. When a new religion comes along, especially one that is inherently evangelical in its need to attract followers, it is prudent to do everything possible to make preceding beliefs look bad, and one good way to do that is to represent the old religion's gods as demons, actively working against the will of the one true God.

So, it makes sense that pagan deities were demonized to make way for Christianity, but why Pan specifically? Why not Zeus, or Apollo? This is only a hypothesis, but there seem to be a couple of logical reasons why Pan would make a good—pardon the pun—scapegoat. First, Pan represents wildness, lust, chaos, and disorder, a marked contrast to the asceticism championed by early Christianity. Second, the fact that Pan looks like an animal makes him easier to convert into a villain. Animals can be viewed as base, primitive, unsophisticated, lacking the morals or philosophy that elevate mankind above the beasts, as well as slaves to raw instinct. It would be more difficult to take a shining figure known for his devotion to logic and reason, such as Apollo, and get people to hate and fear him.

Medievalist and self-proclaimed expert on witchcraft Montague Summers (about whom we will have much to say later) believes that our modern understanding of the Devil's appearance derives from the Greco-Roman god Hephaestus, as well as the Norse trickster Loki. In his introduction to the witch-hunting manual, the *Malleus Maleficarum*, Summers writes:

The worship of Hephaestus in later days seems to have degenerated and to have been identified with some of the secret cults of the evil powers. This was probably due to his connexion with fire and also to his extreme ugliness, for he was frequently represented as a swarthy man of grim and forbidding aspect. It should further be noted that the Italian deity Volcanus, with whom he was to be identified, is the god of destructive fire—fire considered in its rage and terror, as contrasted with fire which is a comfort to the human race, the kindly blaze on the hearth, domestic fire, presided over by the gracious lady Vesta. It is impossible not to think of the fall of Lucifer when one considers the legend of Hephaestus. ....

...Hephaestus, especially in later days, is represented with one leg shortened to denote his lameness; and throughout the Middle

Ages it was popularly believed that his cloven hoof was the one feature which the devil was unable to disguise. In this connexion Loki, the Vulcan of Northern Europe, will be readily remembered. Frederick Hall writes: "Hephaestus, Vulcan, and Loki, each lame from some deformity of foot, in time joined natures with the Pans and satyrs of the upper world; the lame sooty blacksmith donned their goatlike extremities of cloven hoofs, tail, and horns; and the black dwarfs became uncouth ministers of this sooty, black, foul fiend. If ever mortal man accepted the services of these cunning metalworkers, it was for some sinister purpose, and at a cruel price—no less than that of the soul itself, bartered away in a contract of red blood, the emblem of life and the color of fire."[21]

The third reason why I believe the image of Pan was used to represent the Devil was his universality. Horned deities symbolizing the hunt, the elemental forces of nature, and masculine potency were not unique to the Greeks, but were common in many pre-Christian polytheist cultures. The Welsh had their Horned God, made famous in Lloyd Alexander's series of fantasy novels, *The Chronicles of Prydain*, where he is again represented as a villain. In Ireland, a similar deity was known as Cernunnos, again sporting an impressive set of horns and symbolizing the powers of nature. A third representation is found across Britain going by names such as Bucca, Pwca, or Puck (the latter of which has been immortalized by William Shakespeare.)

According to Cornish folklorist Gemma Garry, the Bucca was an ancient horned god resembling a goat, and frequently referred to by traditional witches, healers, or wise women as The Old One or "the devil." It is important to note that the word devil here was never considered as synonymous with the Christian Satan, or with demons in general. The Bucca was old, primordial, a little dangerous (like all gods), and a bit of a trickster, but he certainly wasn't evil. He was just one of a pantheon of polytheistic and household gods called upon for help by workers of traditional magic, and an intrinsic part of the ancient folk beliefs of Britain.

None of these gods were ever identified with wickedness by those who believed in them, but neither were they to be trifled with. They carried an unmistakable air of mystery and danger about them, as one would expect from an ancient nature deity. A hunter might catch sight of one shrouded in mist and shadow in a dark forest glen, a sight sure to send shivers up anyone's spine.

Given all this, it seems only natural that Satan should have horns. It was an image that would capitalize on the primordial fear of nature, while at the same time explicitly casting judgment on the old religions — those that refused to conform with the new Christian status quo — as inherently evil.

Over time, other features got added to Satan's archetypical appearance. He was given bat wings, probably because he needed to be able to fly and because bats are scary, nocturnal creatures that are more dangerous than birds. The pitchfork is a weapon typical of rural, agricultural communities, as opposed to the more sophisticated knives and swords of city-dwellers, again drawing a contrast between the old-fashioned and nature worshipping pagans and the urban Christians. That the Latin word *paganus* literally means a country dweller is again surely no coincidence.

Satan, as powerful as he is, was not expected to shoulder this burden of killing off old religions alone. If you comb through the Bible looking for the names of demons, what you will find is a laundry list of ancient Middle Eastern deities reclassified as devils by the Jewish tribes intent on regarding worship of any god but Yahweh as wicked idolatry. It is worth noting that in the first commandment handed down to Moses at Mount Sinai, Yahweh does not say "there is no God but me" but rather "thou shalt have no other God but me", implying that other gods do in fact exist, they just ought to be avoided.

No One Expected the Spanish Inquisition

Known by modern pagans as "The Burning Times", the years following the late fifteenth century are so notoriously bloodthirsty towards witches that many of their features are common knowledge more than five hundred years later. And while the Spanish Inquisition made famous by Monty Python's Flying Circus was comparatively mild, efforts to root out heresy in other countries deserved their reputation.

In 1467, the first book ever published on witchcraft was written by Alphonsus de Spina. He regarded witchcraft as a delusion, pointing to some bizarre rites in which women adore a wild boar by kissing its hindquarters. The overlap between witch-hunting and the persecution of mental illness will be more thoroughly treated in a later chapter.

Less than two decades after de Spina, however, the Church's attitude towards witchcraft had crystallized into something much more sinister. In 1484, the Bull of Pope Innocent VIII identified witches as a major threat to Catholicism, and gave license to inquisitors to hunt down and prosecute the alleged servants of the devil. Two years later, two inquisitors named Heinrich Kramer and James Sprenger wrote and published what would become the definition witch hunting manual, *Malleus Maleficarum*, The Hammer of Witches.

The title is appropriately blunt and brutal to the subject matter. The book is an exceedingly unpleasant read, deeply rooted in an inexplicable and seemingly all-consuming misogyny. The authors repeatedly attribute to women all the worst vices, describing them as scheming, dishonest, manipulative, envious, petty, and most of all, sexually voracious. It is these vices, they claim, that make women so susceptible to the devil's temptations. In no less than two chapters, Kramer and Sprenger go into lurid detail about the ways in which witches were allegedly plotting to separate unsuspecting men from their genitalia, perhaps giving a clue to the nature of the particular neuroses that inspired this book.

"All witchcraft comes from carnal lust, which is in women insatiable,"[22] declares the Hammer. Indeed, it appears that a hatred and fear of female sexuality in general lies behind a great deal of Catholic witch hysteria. Throughout the work, the authors identify with witches, women who fail to observe taboos against fornication, adultery, and abortion, as well as castigating midwives "who surpass all others in wickedness."[23] The use of medicinal herbs is also condemned, giving one the impression of a general resentment against anyone practicing medicine other than certain approved, male doctors.

While sexual nonconformity is a major focus of the work, it is not the only one. Later, in a section detailing how legal proceedings are to be brought against witches, the authors give an example of how suspicion of heresy and witchcraft might fall on certain members of the community:

As an example of simple heresy, if people are to be found meeting together for the purpose of secret worship, or differing in their manner of life or behavior from the usual habits of the faithful; or if they meet together in sheds or barns, or at the more Holy Seasons in the remoter fields or woods, by day or by night, or are in any way found to separate themselves and not attend to Mass at the usual times or in the usual manner, or form secret friendships with suspected witches: such people incur at least a light suspicion of heresy, because it is proved that heretics often act in this manner.[24]

In other words, any behavior deemed at all out of the ordinary could be grounds for suspicion of witchcraft, and as the book later explains, even light suspicion was no laughing matter. With luck, a person who admitted their error and swore never to engage in heresy again might get away with a warning, but for repeat offenders or the impenitent, anything from imprisonment, to torture, and even death is prescribed as appropriate punishment.

The *Malleus* was extremely popular, and regrettably served as the blueprint for witch-hunters all over the world. As late as 1948 it was described by its translator, Montague Summers (about whom we will have more to say later), as "among the most important, weightiest, and wisest books in the world."[25]

During the prime years of witch-hunting, due process was relaxed considerably due to the difficulty of actually proving the existence of witchcraft. As Jean Bodin, a French jurist and influential writer on witchcraft admitted in 1580:

> *Wherefore it is that one accused of being a witch ought never be fully acquitted and set free unless the calumny of the accuser is clearer than the sun, inasmuch as the proof of such crimes is so obscure and so difficult that not one witch in a million would be accused or punished if the procedure were governed by the ordinary rules.*[26]

This relaxation of the standards of evidence has often been accompanied by a disturbing, though not unpredictable phenomenon: the utilization of witch trials to settle private grudges. Once it is established within a community that an accusation is all that is required to bring about public condemnation, exile, torture, and sometimes even death, it is not surprising that some petty and vindictive minds will use this fact to their advantage, fabricating the symptoms of bewitchment and pointing the finger at a personal enemy or rival. Almost invariably, these cases involve children, who are capable of nourishing the most passionate hatred over the most trivial of slights, and who lack either the understanding to realize the full consequences of their actions or the empathy to care.

One such case involved a Scottish girl named Christine Shaw. In 1696, towards the end of the days of witch-related hysteria in England, the eleven-year-old Christine had a public altercation with another girl, Katherine Campbell, and a local old woman, Agnes Naismith. Shortly thereafter, Christine began exhibiting violent fits, in which she accused Katherine and Agnes of tormenting her with evil spells. She was also in the habit of spitting up small items, bones and pins and bits of clay, that she claimed had been magically placed inside her stomach by her oppressors. As time went on, she began to accuse others in the community, the wiliest of which deflected the accusations by claiming that they themselves were also victims, pointing the finger at still others. By the time a trial could be held, twenty-one people had been implicated in witchcraft. It is notable that the accused here tended to be people of low status, bearing some peculiarity of body or character, and therefore least able to defend themselves on reputational grounds. Apart from Agnes, who was said to have a bad reputation in the community, Christine accused a beggar, a "squint eyed" boy, and several defenseless children.

The following year, the trial convicted seven of the accused, and they were hanged and burned as punishment for their alleged sorcery. Christine recovered from her fits at once, to the surprise of no one. Upon retrospective analysis, she was given the title of the Bargarran Imposter, and nineteenth century investigators discovered a secret hole in the wall near her bed, through which they theorized that the bones and pins could have been passed to her by an accomplice.

The well-known case of the Salem Witch Trials provides another example of young girls leveling accusations of witchcraft, although whether for attention, careless fun, or some personal grudge remains unclear. In the repressive atmosphere of puritan seventeenth century Massachusetts, it's possible that they intended to excuse their own bad behavior through the scapegoating of others. Eight girls between the ages of 12 and 18 began the trouble, manifesting strange behavior, screaming fits, and odd physical postures that the highly religious locals were happy to interpret as bewitchment. When asked about the identity of the witches, "the girls named first the obvious scapegoats of the community, the vulnerable and weak—Tituba the Negro slave; Sarah Good, the pipe-smoking beggar; and Sarah Osborne, a thrice-wedded cripple. Martha Cory, the fourth to be accused, had an illegitimate half-caste son."[27]

Two of the accusers later recanted their claims of bewitchment, but not in time to prevent Salem from becoming the most notorious example of mass hysteria in history, in which 25 people were ultimately killed on suspicion of witchcraft.

The extent to which anything out of the ordinary could be taken as evidence of witchcraft can be seen taken to a ridiculous extreme in the theories of the witch hunter La Sieur Bouvet, who held that even the ability to withstand torture better than others must be a sign of diabolic influence. Bouvet claimed that it was absurd to attribute such resilience to simple fortitude or hardiness, and that the only possible explanation was the use of some magical charm, which he suggested be found by a thorough search of the accused's body, the burning off of all hair and, if that failed, the administration of a strong emetic to induce vomiting, the assumption being that the witch had swallowed some magical protective charm. Here again we encounter the "no win" scenario in which capitulation to torture and confession, as well as resistance to torture and denial, are regarded as equally damning forms of evidence.

Abnormality need not even be physical in order to be condemned and punished. This is a subject with which we will deal in greater depth in a later chapter, particularly as it pertains to mental illness, but here it is enough to say that some authorities, notable among them the philosopher Thomas

Hobbes, professed a disbelief in witchcraft, yet nevertheless approved of witch trails and persecutions on the grounds that the mere *belief* in one's own supernatural abilities and the attempt to make use of them was sufficient to warrant punishment. In other words, Hobbes thought someone who believed herself a witch, even if such a belief was mere delusion, should be treated as though she had actually partnered with the Devil in causing mayhem. This point of view provides a rather shocking glimpse into the psychology of the inquisitor, where privately held, nonconforming thoughts are regarded as equally criminal as actual deeds.

In the early twentieth century, interest in witchcraft was revived somewhat by the enigmatic figure of Montague Summers. Summers was an antiquarian, scholar and eccentric who referred to himself as a priest, but whose clerical credentials historians have found it difficult to identify. He went around dressed in archaic clerical garb, and nurtured a fanatical interest in, and hatred of, all things witch-related. In all probability, he was the last serious scholar to profess a total and unwavering belief in the existence of witches, their relationship with the Devil, and their ability to perform supernatural feats of evil on unsuspecting Christians. The irony of Summers' work is that he was himself the ultimate nonconformist, rebelling tirelessly against the dominant views of the enlightenment in order to carry out his personal crusade against the forces of darkness.

And yet, we should be grateful to Summers, for in spite of his questionable grip on reality, he managed to produce several volumes of exquisite scholarship on the subjects of vampires, werewolves, and other creatures of the dark. Displaying a fluency in multiple languages, dead and living, and a remarkable attention to detail, his works survive as invaluable references to any modern scholars interested in these esoteric topics. It is also somewhat refreshing to read a scholarly study on werewolves by someone who, rather than snidely scoffing at the naivety of popular folklore, treats his subject with the respect and sincerity of one who is one hundred percent convinced that vampires and werewolves are literally real, and pose a tangible threat to society at large.

For our purposes, the most relevant of Summers' many books is his *History of Witchcraft and Demonology*. In it, Summers employs his prodigious scholarship to pull together what he considers to be the "evidence" for witchcraft from an impressive variety of sources, ancient and modern, in a variety of languages, dead and living. His description of the Witches Sabbat, fictional though it may be, is not to be missed for the sheer color and terror he manages to infuse into the subject. By the twentieth century, most Christians had come to regard the Inquisition as something of an embarrassment, a relic of bygone days when overzealous cardinals were given free rein to persecute the innocent. Not so, Summers. He makes it clear that the Inquisition has his wholehearted approval, his only regret being that it stopped too soon. He speaks with approval of the days when "holiest pontiffs and wisest judges, grave philosopher and discreet scholar, king and peasant, careless noble and earnest divine, all alike were of one mind in the prosecution of sorcery." And how "unhesitatingly and perseveringly man sought to stamp out the plague with the most terrible of all penalties, the cautery of fire." He also cautions against judging these aforesaid prosecutors as mad fanatics, as history at that time, and indeed today, is likely to do.

The Boy Who Lived

The most recent flare up of anti-witch hysteria stems from the immense popularity of the Harry Potter series of books and movies. The story of a young boy who attends a wizarding school, discovers he has amazing powers, and ultimately must lead the fight of good versus evil, captured the imagination of the world and quickly became one of the most successful franchises in history. It's not hard to see why: the story makes expert use of traditional archetypes and storytelling tropes including, but not limited to, wish fulfillment, the chosen one, escapism, a battle for the soul of mankind, novelty, immersive world building, great characters, boarding school, childhood rebellion and coming of age, friendship, the rule of three, terrifying villains and convincing danger, the wise old sage, the call to adventure, and on and on.

Naturally, not everyone was happy about the success of J.K. Rowling's creation. Various religious groups, but primarily evangelical Christianity, took issue with what they considered to be a promotion of witchcraft. They called for the books to be banned in schools and libraries, and some even resorted to burning them, citing the biblical verses against all forms of magic. The organization Focus on the Family was a particularly prominent critic of Pottermania.

While it is true that J.K. Rowling, having done her homework, includes numerous references to actual historical figures— alchemists, occultists and natural philosophers—and practices, the idea that the magic depicted in the Harry Potter series bears any resemblance to the actual religion of Wicca or related faiths is pretty ridiculous. In the books, characters cast spells by waving magic wands and shouting faux-Latin incantations. This allows them to perform impossible feats such as causing objects to levitate, creating light from darkness, or even killing enemies. In the real world, witchcraft-based religions tend to be far more devotional, with spellcasting, when it occurs at all, resembling organized prayer more than anything else.

We can happily note that these denunciations came from a vocal, but very small, minority. One poll found that just seven percent of adults who had heard of the books held a negative opinion of them. It's unclear to what extent these negative opinions were based on religious grounds, rather than on simple literary taste.

The Harry Potter series remains, like *The Lord of the Rings* or *The Chronicles of Narnia,* a harmless, though uncommonly well-crafted, bit of fantasy literature. But lingering anxieties over witchcraft, ignorance of pagan faiths, and a knee-jerk rejection of that which is alien and difficult to understand attracts persecutors even in these comparatively enlightened times.

Chapter 6

Medical Maladies

The expectation of conformity is not limited to behavior alone. It also extends to physical appearance, and those who look different can expect precious little appreciation for their deviation from the norm. In a sense, this is understandable. Once again, evolutionary biology dictates our instinctual reactions. The species benefits from passing along healthy genes while screening out those which may cause a disadvantage to our progeny if passed on. This is why we are attracted to symmetrical faces, athletic bodies, and indicators of fertility. On the other hand, there is an instinctive repulsion to disease, deformity, and weakness in general.

Of course, as civilized people, it is incumbent upon us to resist these instincts and not judge people based solely upon their looks. Today, we recognize that the full measure of a human being has little to do with external appearance. To do otherwise is to risk repeating the horrors of the eugenics movement, in which a zeal for scientific advancement unmitigated by concern for minority rights or simple human decency, led to tens of thousands of involuntary sterilizations in early twentieth century America. In the end, it took a confrontation with Nazi Germany for the rest of world to come to terms with how dangerous it is to judge people by the way they look or their racial characteristics or history.

Still, the tendency to ascribe demonic or magical characteristics to someone based on their appearance runs deep in the culture. If asked, any child can tell you what a witch looks like. She is an old woman with a long, crooked nose and warts. Despite attempts to rehabilitate the witch's image with attractive "good" witches like Glinda from the Wizard of Oz or Hermione from Harry Potter, the archetype of the withered crone still looms large in the modern psyche.

Men get off easier, but we still hear instances of odd-looking folks being described as goblin-like, trollish, or elfish, although this last is not generally intended to be derogatory. Deformity too, comes with its own stereotypes. People of restricted growth have traditionally been likened to elves, dwarves, and leprechauns. There is the sense that because they are different, there must be something magical about them. In fiction, deformed characters occupy a certain role which is usually at least somewhat antagonistic. The Phantom of the Opera is driven underground by his facial scars, where he becomes bitter and alienated from society. The Hunchback of Notre Dame, though written as a sympathetic character worthy of pity and empathy in the original novel, has since come to be lumped in with the "monsters" of the classic film era, being awkwardly shoehorned in with the likes of Frankenstein and Dracula. There's little mention of a *physical* transformation from Dr. Jekyll to Mr. Hyde in Robert Louis Stevenson's original novel, which deals more with split personalities and the repressed impulses of the subconscious, but in every adaptation to visual media, the good doctor's evil half is portrayed as short, unkempt, and ugly, a visual representation of his moral character. The unfortunate Joker, the Batman villain, is transformed from a small-time crook into an insane super villain by suffering physical scarring from a vat of acid. In the classic Star Trek episode "Mirror, Mirror", Evil Spock had a goatee, differentiating him from his wholesome, clean-shaven counterpart. While these characters are often unpleasant figures who commit horrible atrocities, the point is that their physical appearance is used as part of their identity, as frequently as a self-explanatory source for their villainy.

Before the advent of modern medicine, when life was hard and weakness introduced into a family or tribe could represent a serious drain on resources, it was not uncommon for families to deal preemptively with deformity by employing the concept of the "changeling". In folklore, a changeling is a child from the fairy world that has been swapped with a human baby. Fairies, it was said, liked human children and would take almost any opportunity to steal them, substituting their own offspring in their place, and therefore babies had to be carefully guarded and protective measures taken to prevent such a crime from occurring.

It was fairly easy to tell whether you were the victim of such a swap, for fairy babies are quite different from human ones. They are irritable and ill-tempered, often aggressive to the point of violence. In appearance they tend to be shriveled, like an old man, and may have deformities like extra fingers or toes, and misshapen facial features. If allowed to grow older, changelings were generally lacking in basic human emotions such as empathy and kindness, generally proving very unpleasant children indeed.

The belief in changelings justified a mother quickly and quietly disposing of an unwanted offspring. In fact, it was standard practice that changelings should be thrown into a river and drowned before they could be allowed to cause any serious trouble. The fact that the child was supposedly not related to its parents, but instead the spawn of fairies, alleviated the guilt and social stigma that would otherwise come with infanticide.

As with so many of the examples in this book, there were practical reasons why such a practice might come about. Caring for a severely disabled child could impose a serious hardship on a family already barely able to make ends meet, and so labeling it a changeling and disposing of it would have been considered a mercy for all parties involved. On the other hand, once such an excuse is available, we can expect that it would be abused. It is likely that plenty of children were killed simply because they looked strange, had a difficult temperament, or maybe to dispose of the evidence of an extramarital affair.

Throughout the nineteenth century, the now-debunked pseudoscience of physiognomy attempted to make predictions about individual behavior and tendencies by examining the facial features. Claims that there existed such a thing as a criminal "type" of skull shape or facial structure were common, and that you could rely on individuals manifesting those features to be bad eggs, even if their behavior thus far showed no evidence of wrongdoing. Even in the age of scientific discovery, we couldn't escape the sense that "badness" must manifest itself in uncommon physical appearance. Oscar Wilde's *The Picture of Dorian Gray* tells of a magical painting which ages and decays over time, leaving the subject unchanged. When the title character starts committing wicked deeds, the figure in the painting becomes visibly distorted, its features becoming hard and cruel while its hands acquire the red tint of blood. The assumption here is that bad actions cannot help but leave a visible imprint behind, and that conversely, we can tell the bad actor based on the way he looks.

Deformity or disease as an excuse for demonization may actually explain the origin of many of the myths that inspire modern day horror movies. There is a reason to believe that stories of vampires and werewolves may have at least something to do with then-unexplained bodily illnesses, rather than pure flights of imaginative fancy.

Porphyria is a rare congenital disease involving a defect in bone marrow. The symptoms are many and various, but they include a sensitivity to light, jaundiced skin, reddish teeth, deformities of the nose and ears, and occasionally an excess of bodily or facial hair. Porphyria is frequently accompanied by mental disturbances such as hysteria, manic depression, or epilepsy. In an essay reprinted from a medical journal in an anthology discussing the phenomenon of werewolfism, the author writes:

It is possible, then, to paint a picture of a porphyric which, though not necessarily characteristic or typical, will fit with all the available evidence in the literature of porphyria: such a person, because of photosensitivity and the resultant disfigurement, may choose only to wander about at night. The pale, yellowish, excoriated skin may be explained by the haemolytic anaemia, jaundice, and pruritis. These features, together with hypertrichosis and pigmentation, fit well with the descriptions, in older literature, of werewolves. The unhappy person may be mentally disturbed, and show some type or degree of abnormal behaviour. In ancient times this would be accentuated by the physical and social treatment he received from the other villagers, whose instincts would be to explain the apparition in terms of witchcraft or Satanic possession.[28]

Given the above list of symptoms, it is equally easy to imagine the porphyriac as the inspiration for the belief in vampires as well, with the reddish hue of the teeth and gums giving the suggestion of a creature which feeds on blood.

Josh McDowell and Don Stewart are two Christian writers who believe that any practices approaching "the occult" are wicked and dangerous; they nevertheless offer two further suggestions for medical conditions that might once have been mistaken for demonic possession, witchcraft, or the undead:

Huntington's Chorea is a disease that does not show up in most of its victims until they are past thirty years of age. This disease causes the victim to behave in a peculiar manner, including involuntary body movements, fits of anger and irritability and a loss of intelligence.

The victim may make strange outbursts of laughter, cry like a baby or talk endlessly. It can easily be seen how a sufferer could be mistaken for being bewitched or being a witch. Huntington's Chorea is also an inherited disease which would convince the superstitious that the bewitchment had been passed to the children.

Tourette's Syndrome is a rare disease which usually begins in childhood. The victim experiences tics—involuntary muscle movements—throughout the body but especially in the face. The sufferer may also kick and stamp his feet. Along with making awful faces, the victim makes involuntary noises which include shouts, grunts, and swearing. All of these symptoms are beyond the control of the sufferer but appear to the uneducated as being a sign of being a witch, possessed by the devil.[29]

The aforementioned *Malleus Maleficarum* notes that witches can be identified by their inability to shed tears, even when subjected to torture. In fact, such a condition can be more readily explained by dry eyes resulting from, among other things, a vitamin deficiency (likely common in fifteenth century Europe) than by some secret pact with the devil.

Of course, all of the above amounts to speculation. We can't say for a fact that these or similar medical conditions contributed to fear of witches, werewolves, and vampires, but it seems extremely likely that in times when medical science was in its infancy and belief in the supernatural was widespread that plenty of victims of horrible, disfiguring diseases were made to suffer the added hardship of being regarded as an instrument of the Devil. As in the other cases we've looked at, the mere fact of looking or behaving differently, in a way that failed to conform to the expectations of society at large, inspired not pity, not understanding, but fear and hatred.

Demonizing the Abnormal Mind

"The Devil made me do it" is an excuse even older and more well-worn than "the dog ate my homework", and just like its more modern-day equivalent, it is unlikely to get anyone off the hook for a misdeed. In fact, you are likely to get into more trouble, not less, if you manage to convince anyone that malevolent spirits are using your body as an instrument of mischief.

For most of human history, aberrant behavior was about as likely to be explained by demonic possession as by anything else. People fear what they don't understand, and if a person's appearance, actions, or demeanor seems foreign or incomprehensible, even if it is not hostile or overtly harmful, it can be tempting to turn to demons as an explanation. One of the characteristics of human beings is that we are all different, and some of us are *really* different, so different that our neighbors have difficulty even recognizing our lifestyles as valid. When that happens, the nonconformist tends to get slapped with a label that makes him easier to understand. Nowadays, these labels are more likely to relate to physical or mental illness, but it wasn't that long ago when demonic possession would serve as an acceptable explanation.

Psychiatrist Thomas Szasz sums up this attitude:

Western tradition sanctions interpreting insanity in religious terms, attributing it to demonic possession, treating it by means of exorcism, and accepting clerical coercion as morally laudable and legitimate. When people believed that an eternal life in the hereafter was more important than a brief sojourn on earth, exorcizing the possessed person by torturing him, to improve the quality of his life after death, was perceived as an act of beneficence.[30]

The New Testament contains several accounts of demonic possession, in which Jesus' ability to cast out or exorcize evil spirits is given as evidence for his divinity. The descriptions of the afflicted persons are telling. In the Gospel According to Mark, Jesus is confronted by a man exhibiting great strength and erratic behavior.

He lived among the tombs; and no one could restrain him anymore, not even with a chain. For he had often been restrained with

shackles and chains, but the chains he wrenched apart, and the
shackles he broke in pieces, and no one had the strength to subdue
him. Night and day among the tombs and on the mountains he was
always howling and bruising himself with stones.[31]

Jesus subsequently heals the man with an exorcism, but the symptoms described here recall our earlier descriptions of suspected werewolves.

In the Gospel According to Matthew, Jesus heals a young boy who is said to be "lunatic and sore vexed, and ofttimes he falleth into the fire, and oft into the water."[32] In another passage, the boy is also said to be foaming at the mouth, gnashing his teeth, and pining listlessly away. Perhaps most importantly, the boy is said to inspire fear in others.[33] Again, these symptoms are explained as the work of evil demons rather than as a naturally occurring problem with an abnormal mind. A third example has Jesus cure a mute and blind man whose afflictions are believed to be the work of demons.[34]

What all these examples have in common is that symptoms of a medical or behavioral nature are ascribed to evil spirits who can cause not only bodily illness, but aberrant acts as well. The Bible, as well as apocryphal scriptures, contain quite a few more narratives of demonic possession, but belief in this phenomenon was not limited to the early Common era. Throughout the Middle Ages, the Catholic Church listed such phenomena as speaking in tongues, displaying great strength, possessing inaccessible knowledge, blasphemy, profanity, and fits of psychotic rage as telltale signs that the Devil was at work within a human body. Notable cases of demonic possession continued well into the twentieth century, with several of these being made into sensational horror films to shock and delight the public. The common factor is that deviant behavior is explained or excused by the claim that the guilty party is either voluntarily or involuntarily cooperating with some form of evil spirit.

With the advance of medical science, the tendency to attribute unusual symptoms to demonic interference decreased along with a better understanding of the natural causes of disease. In a feat of creative logic typical for the would be witch-hunter, Montague Summers attempts to turn this tendency on his head. While he admits that some cases of alleged possession may have in fact been the result of misdiagnosis, he simultaneously offers up this conundrum in defense of the Bible's accuracy:

> *That the demoniacs were often afflicted with other diseases as well is highly probable. The demons may have attacked those who were already sick, whilst the very fact of obsession or possession would of itself produce disease as a natural consequence.*[35]

One cannot help but be reminded of the Inquisitorial trial by ordeal, in which the accused's ability to survive is taken as proof of her guilt. Here, Summers suggests that the presence of natural disease, rather than ruling out demonic possession, actually strengthens the evidence *for* supernatural afflictions. Faced with such tortured reasoning, it becomes difficult or impossible for the abnormal person to deny any association with the powers of darkness. This kind of logical trap is popular among the self-appointed arbiters of normalcy, and we will see it crop up again in the case of modern mental illness, where professions of sanity are interpreted as nothing more than the mind's inability to grasp its own defects.

For a more charitable, but no less supernatural interpretation of strange behavior, consider this passage from Dion Fortune's *Psychic Self-Defense*. Fortune was a psychologist and occultist writing in the first half of the twentieth century, and was one of the first to connect Jungian theories about the subconscious to the subjective experiences of those who practiced the occult or studied the paranormal. Here she is describing certain types of people who can prove a dangerous or negative influence on those who are emotionally vulnerable.

There are many of us who have met people who might well be described as nonhuman, soulless, in that the ordinary human motives are not operative with them, nor do the ordinary human feelings prompt or inhibit them. We cannot but love them, for they have great charm, but we cannot but dread them as well, for they spread an infinitude of suffering around them. Although seldom deliberately evil, they are singularly detrimental to all with whom they come in contact. They, for their part, are unhappy and lonely in our midst. They feel themselves to be alien and uncompanioned; every man's hand is against them, and in consequence it all too often happens that their hand is against everyone and they develop a puckish malevolence, though there is seldom calculated evil-doing. Gratitude, compassion, good faith, morality, and common honesty are utterly foreign to their natures, as far beyond their conception as the differential calculus. They are not immoral, however, but simply non-moral. On the other hand, they possess the virtues of absolute sincerity and great courage. In terms of human ethics they are "undesirables," but they have an ethic of their own to which they are loyal, and that is the beauty which is truth, and this is all they know, and, as far as their life is concerned, all they need to know. In appearance they are usually small and slight, possessing unusual physical strength and endurance but very liable to nervous exhaustion and brain-storms. In social relations they take violent likes and dislikes; they have a facile and demonstrative affection towards those they like, but quickly forget them. Gratitude and pity are unknown to their nature. Towards those they dislike they are pettily malicious, and in all relations of life they are utterly irresponsible. One cannot describe them better than to say that they resemble nothing so much as a blend of Persian kitten and pet monkey. They have the beauty and aloofness and charm of the cat, and the amusing, mischievous destructiveness of the monkey.

Many human beings hate them at sight; others are fascinated by them because they bring with them a sense of unearthly beauty and a quickening of the life-forces.[36]

There can be little doubt that Fortune was describing people that we would now classify as sociopaths or psychopaths. Unaccountably born without the emotions of empathy or compassion (or perhaps having these emotions driven from them through early childhood abuse), sociopaths and psychopaths are often described as glib, charming, manipulative, mercurial, cunning, devious, and prone to malevolence. Contrary to their portrayal in movies and television, most people diagnosed with sociopathy or psychopathy are not serial killers or career criminals. While perhaps not inhibited from violence by the sort of inner conscience the rest of us have, they nevertheless recognize the practical value of peaceful cooperation and integration into the community. Sociopaths tend to be goal-oriented, and it is dramatically harder to accomplish your goals when constantly having to be on the run from the police. It is therefore the case that sociopaths tend to do well in business and politics more often than they end up on America's Most Wanted.

It is nevertheless true that psychopaths, as Fortune notes above, tend to inspire fear and hatred in those who manage to work out their true natures. Again, there is something instinctual in being repulsed by those who possess a value system so different from our own, and who lack the same inhibitions we have. It is worth noting that Fortune uses the terms "nonhuman" and "soulless" to describe these people, regarding them, like the changelings described above, as coming from some kind of parallel fairy world. There can hardly be a greater example of nonconformity than refusal to participate in the basic human emotions that are shared across every culture and time period, so it is not surprising that these individuals would tend to be regarded as some kind of malevolent spirit rather than simply a different sort of human being.

Another type of human who has been subject to systematic demonization over the years are those who engage in homosexual activity. Dating back to its prohibition in the Book of Leviticus, through the story of Sodom and Gomorrah, all the way up until the twentieth century, homosexuality has not only been regarded as something unnatural, but morally evil as well.

There is an interesting pattern in the commandments of the Old Testament, where advice that appears to have been purely pragmatic in nature has, over time, becomes interpreted as morally imperative. For example, the prohibition on eating pork and shellfish likely originated as advice to prevent the spread of food-borne illness. The prohibition against mixing cloth made from different fibers in the same garment was probably an instruction to avoid producing inferior textiles. The taboo against incest (which predates the Old Testament and is common to all cultures) is designed to maintain a healthy and diverse gene pool and reduce the deformities that result from inbreeding. With this in mind, it seems likely that the prohibitions on homosexuality and masturbation were put in place in order to encourage more pregnancy, and therefore more childbirth. More children means more labor to help the tribe, more warriors to protect it, and a greater chance of carrying on its religion, values, and culture into the future. A society with too much homosexuality and not enough heterosexuality could well find itself going extinct in a couple of generations.

Somehow or other—most likely because the commandments came from a supposedly omnibenevolent God—these guides for practical living became tangled up with the idea of sin, and those who broke the commandments became regarded as servants of the Devil and his evil machinations. Homosexuals, therefore, became sinners, forced to conceal their natural inclinations under a cloud of shame and fear—shame that their very thoughts and emotions were transgressions against the almighty, and fear that they might be persecuted, tortured, or even killed if anyone found out their secret. As late as the twentieth century, the Nazis under Hitler and the Cubans under Che Guevara and Fidel Castro confined homosexuals to camps where they were systematically executed. Even today, there are large swaths of the globe where openly gay people have good reason to fear for their safety.

Even in the comparatively enlightened United States, homosexuality was regarded as a mental illness, appearing in the Diagnostic and Statistical Manual used by psychiatrists to diagnose disorders, until the astonishingly late date of 1987. Until that time, it was perfectly acceptable to subject gay Americans to all sorts of involuntary treatment, from conversion therapy, to drugging, to the barbarism of electroshock or insulin shock therapies, all in the name of "curing" them of their alleged disease and making them "normal" like everyone else. Now that homosexuality has finally won some acceptance as a different, but not inferior, way of existing, we still hear accusations that transgenderism and other minority sexualities are, in fact, mental illnesses, and those that suffer from them ought to be treated whether they like it or not. *Plus ça change, plus c'est la même chose.* Indeed, the label "mental illness" has become little more than a modern euphemism for demonic possession.

The Psychiatric Inquisition
We have dealt in detail with the practices of the Inquisition in seeking out and destroying witches, as defined by beliefs or actions which contradicted the official doctrines of the Church. But while the methods and motives of the Inquisition are today generally met with retrospective disapproval, a surprisingly parallel form of persecution has been allowed to progress through the centuries comparatively unchallenged.

Today, the pursuit of mental health is a societal obsession

almost akin to a religion of its own. Psychiatrists are keen to label any abnormal pattern of behavior or thought as a "disorder" and to take measures which could frequently be described as drastic to aid in the restoration of sanity. If the most recent edition of the Diagnostic and Statistical Manual, the go-to sourcebook for psychiatric disorders, is to be believed, Americans not suffering from some kind of mental illness are fast in danger of becoming their own minority, a concept that would have once been inconceivable even to the most zealous medical professionals. Of course, any talk about the mind being "ill", "disordered" or "abnormal" presumes a model, even a hypothetical one, of an ideal mind. What would a "well," "orderly" and "normal" mind look like, and if a majority of individuals suffers from a disorder, does it even make sense to talk about normality as a useful concept?

These are difficult questions, but they have not stopped psychiatrists from enthusiastically diving in with all manner of prescriptive techniques to enforce their vision of mental health upon the rest of us, whether we like it or not. Mental illness is, after all, a form of nonconformity. The so-called patient holds beliefs which are not held by others, hears sounds that others cannot hear, sees visions that others cannot see, experiences emotional states, alien to others, behaves in ways which others consider odd or illogical. The person who gambles, drinks, or smokes "too much" is said to be an addict. The person who eats "too little" is said to be anorexic. The person who washes his hands "too often" is said to be compulsive. The person who is "too sad" is said to be depressed. The person who experiences sensations others do not experience is said to be schizophrenic. The person who holds beliefs others do not hold is said to be delusional.

It is worth noting, looking back at Chapter 4, that Saints and other holy figures throughout history very commonly eat too little, pray too much, hold strange beliefs, witness peculiar visions, and experience exalted emotional states that many people would find alarming. That history has labeled such people not as dangerous lunatics, but as saintly figures deserving of awe and reverence reveals the truth about mental illness: that it is fundamentally a political concept rather than a medical one. Whether thinkers in the extreme minority are considered madmen or men of genius depends heavily on the socio-political context of the time, and on our retrospective historical understanding of those same factors.

Regardless of which camp a particular individual is likely to fall into, it generally makes little difference in terms of persecution and demonization. As we have seen, strange behaviors were once thought to be caused by the actions of literal demons working their mischief through a human vessel. As religious attitudes changed and mankind began to adopt a more scientific worldview, these demons were replaced by invisible, undetectable forces which could either be chemical or social depending on the school of thought one subscribes to. The difference is largely one of semantics, for the implications are the same. The actions of the nonconformist are rarely viewed as a product of his own free will, but are almost always ascribed to some exterior force over which he has little or no control. One might think that such a classification would absolve the offending party of guilt and responsibility. How can we hold a particular behavior against someone, after all, if he is unable to control or change it? The insanity defense in court is predicated on this understanding, holding that criminal punishment of the mentally deficient is a miscarriage of justice. On the other hand, this abdication of personal responsibility has a far more sinister effect than the mere protection of the innocent.

If we are able to write off the actions of the nonconformist as involuntary and irrational, we solve such thorny little problems as medical consent or respect for a person's individual wishes. How, after all, can anyone give, or indeed withhold, consent if he is not in control of his actions, or even of his own mind? Again, one would think that the inability of a person to consent would be a *de facto* prohibition on external interference. The law doesn't regard children as being able to give consent either, but that doesn't mean we can do whatever we want to them in utter disregard for their wishes. The person who infers consent from a child's legal inability to give it is likely to find himself on the wrong side of the law in a hurry. Alas, it would seem that society regards the nonconformist as rather less important than children in this regard. While this state of affairs has admittedly improved in the last few decades, it is still far too common to find people diagnosed with mental illnesses to suffer involuntary imprisonment, relocation, drugging, and other forms of traumatic "treatment", all allegedly for their own good.

Thomas Szasz, a Hungarian psychiatrist who has probably done more to protect the rights of mental patients than any other individual, authored many books on this subject, but the one which best suits our purposes here is entitled *The Manufacture of Madness*. In it, Szasz draws a detailed analogy between the psychiatric movement and the Inquisition's crusade against witches throughout much of the middle ages. Upon examination, it is striking how closely the two accusations "being a witch" and "being mad" resemble one another. Both utilize the presumption of guilt, both demand the victim prove the unprovable in order to absolve herself, both employ as evidence various forms of abnormal behavior that could be explained in any number of ways, and both, upon conviction, rob the accused of any further rights and condemn them to the most terrible forms of torture.

I could easily quote many pages from this remarkable book in service of the analogy, but instead I will content myself with a couple of brief passages, with the strong recommendation that interested readers seek out the original material in its entirety.

Dr. Szasz writes:

The behavior of persons whose conduct differs from that of their fellows—either by falling below the standards of the group or by surpassing them—constitutes a similar mystery and threat [to witchcraft]; the notions of demonic possession and madness supply a primitive theory for explaining such occurrences and appropriate methods for coping with them.[37]

And then, a few pages later:

In the new—secular and "scientific"—climate, as in any other, there were still the disaffected, the disadvantaged, and the men who thought and criticized too much. Conformity was still demanded. The nonconformist, the objector, in short, all who denied or refused to affirm society's dominant values, were still the enemies of society. To be sure, the proper ordering of this new society was no longer conceptualized in terms of Divine Grace; it was viewed in terms of Public Health. Its internal enemies were seen as mad, and Institutional Psychiatry came into being, as had the Inquisition earlier, to protect the group from this threat.[38]

From this it is clear that the motives of Institutional Psychiatry and of the Inquisition were alike in that they were not interested in pursuing truth, health, or indeed salvation, but in enforcing group norms and suppressing any nonconformity that threatened those norms.

Szasz goes on to point out that the primitive conception of disease was twofold: illness could either come from natural or demonic causes. When a natural cause could not be determined, it was assumed that the actions of a malevolent supernatural power were at work, most likely a demon or a witch acting under the authority and power of the Devil. As the scientific progression of the Enlightenment began to regard belief in witches and demons as outmoded and unfashionable, a new model had to emerge for conditions that could still not be explained by observable, physical causes, and thus came about the substitution of the concept of insanity in place of possession or witchcraft. Of course, doctors had no clearer an idea of how to deal with madness than they did with how to drive out demons, so it should come as no surprise that their methods were no less arbitrary or cruel as those of the Inquisition. Ignorance was no deterrent to inventiveness, however, and we therefore see a grotesque parody of the medieval chamber of horrors emerging in so-called mental hospitals, albeit with the false veneer of scientific legitimacy.

Among the treatments imposed upon people who were deemed mad were the following: binding the patient and rendering him immobile for long periods of time; submerging the patient in cold water repeatedly for hours on end; inducing deliberate brain damage through overdoses of insulin; deliberate brain damage inflicted by an ice pick applied to the brain (euphemistically termed "lobotomy"); inducing convulsions through the application of electricity to the patient's head; and inducing compliance and lethargy through psychoactive drugs like lithium or Ritalin. If all else failed, the patient could always be imprisoned for an indefinite period of time, quite likely for the entire remainder of his unfortunate life. Unlike witches, psychiatric patients were seldom granted the mercy of a quick execution.

It is often said, so often in fact as to risk becoming a meaningless platitude, that there is a fine line between genius and madness. In Chapter 3, we examined some men of genius who were persecuted for dreaming up ideas that challenged the orthodox truisms of their times. Here, we see that those with similarly strange ideas risk being subjected to the same fate, absent history's posthumous vindication. In the subjective experience of a person undergoing such treatment, it doubtless makes little difference whether he is being tortured for saying that the Earth goes around the Sun, or for saying that he hears phantom voices telling him that he is the reincarnation of Napoleon. The end result is the same.

This matters, not only for reasons of basic humanity and decency towards our fellow man, but because it is so often the nonconformists who come up with ideas that benefit us as a species. While the would-be Emperor of France may have little to contribute to science or culture, it has been pointed out that great thinkers of all stripes are wont to engage in behaviors that could be charitably deemed "eccentric" and more dogmatically condemned as "pathological." It is doubtful whether Isaac Newton would have developed his theories or gravitation or optics had he been confined to a sanitarium, having pieces of his prodigious brain surgically removed "for his own good." And yet, Newton, along with many of his intellectual peers, was far from what we would consider a normal or typical specimen of humanity.

In his book *Solitude: A Return to the Self*, psychologist Anthony Storr discusses the eccentricities of great artists and thinkers, particularly with respect to their tendency to shun ordinary human relationships. He points out that the temptation by some analysts to label these men of genius as mentally ill, medically abnormal, or otherwise pathological is generally unhelpful and minimizes the benefits of human diversity to society at large. Discussing the cases of Immanuel Kant, Ludwig von Wittgenstein, and Sir Isaac Newton, all of whom exhibit severely nonconformist behavior throughout their lives, he writes:

> *Kant, Wittgenstein, and Newton were all men of genius who, however different they may have been in other ways, shared a vast capacity for original, abstract thought with a lack of close involvement with other human beings. Indeed, it could reasonably be argued that, if they had had wives and families, their achievements*

would have been impossible. For the higher reaches of abstraction demand long periods of solitude and intense concentration which are hard to find if a man is subject to the emotional demands of a spouse and children.

Psycho-analysts will point to the obvious fact that these three men were technically 'abnormal, and I concede that all three exhibited more than the usual share of what is generally deemed 'psycho-pathology'. Nevertheless, all three survived and made important contributions to human knowledge and understanding which, I consider, they could not have made if they had not been predominately solitary.... The psychopathology of such men is no more than an exaggeration of traits which can be found in all of us.[39]

Storr recognizes the tendency for other writers and psychologists to want to demonize nonconformity by labeling it as pathological, as illness, and as somehow dangerous, and rightly points out that without such eccentricities, the world would be infinitely poorer.

In the next chapter, we will look at the way in which some people of exceptional talent and ability have been similarly condemned as the product of sinister and supernatural interference on the part of the Infernal Powers.

Chapter 7

Evil Individualists

From their very beginnings, the American colonies were regarded as eccentric places full of weirdos and oddballs, and with good reason. To undertake the six-week journey across the Atlantic, leaving everything that one knows behind in favor of an uncharted and frequently deadly wilderness would have required an independent streak bordering on madness. Nevertheless, enough people were willing to take that leap that it didn't take long for a new civilization to emerge across the pond that placed an unusual emphasis on individualism and independence. There's a reason why even today the United States manifests a resistance to the kind of collectivist thought that is common in Europe and Asia.

By the time of the nineteenth century, America was well established as an independent culture, with the innovations of the industrial revolution creating a hitherto unheard of ability for individuals to survive and prosper without a reliance on close-knit tribes or extended families. By the middle of the century, the California gold rush had created generations of frontiersmen willing to brave the western wilds for the chance at wealth and glory. The idea of "The Wild West" was born, in which stoic cowboys lived an "every man for himself" existence divorced from civilization as we know it. Jack London wrote gripping tales of grizzled heroes facing the elements in the Yukon with no more company than a pack of dogs, and Herman Melville spun popular tales of long and lonely sea voyages aboard whaling ships. Are all these stories historically accurate? Certainly not, but the point is that nineteenth century America provided a cultural atmosphere for the ideas of individualism to flourish in ways they never had before.

It is not surprising that these cultural and technological changes were accompanied by a philosophical movement. The American Individualists were a small but influential group of thinkers who sought to eschew the confines of society and government in favor of self-expression, spiritual advancement, and the right to be left alone.

After the Civil War, the formerly meager American government had begun to expand at a rate that alarmed some. The war had been costly, with new levels of government spending requiring an income tax for the first time in the country's history. Previously, all revenue had been raised through duties and tariffs on foreign goods, so the idea of a direct tax on income was new to Americans, although they would soon grow used to it. Furthermore, the Federal Government had, for the first time, directly demonstrated its control over the states, by forcibly preventing secession, and with President Lincoln expanding his own powers in disregard of the Constitution. Lincoln famously suspended the writ of *habeas corpus*, and jailed journalists for criticizing the war effort. To those who had grown up in the wilds of a nation conceived in liberty, all of this must have seemed like a threat to their way of life, regardless of how they felt about the war itself.

Two of the most outspoken critics of government at this time were Benjamin Tucker and Lysander Spooner, a cranky old attorney with a long white beard and a razor-sharp pen. He founded his own mail delivery company in an effort to compete with the post office (before being shut down by the government) and wrote extensively about the inherent immorality of the state. His most famous work argues that the Constitution cannot be binding as a legal document, because everyone who signed it was now dead, and men have no legal right to enlist their unborn children into legal agreements without their consent. He also famously likened the state to a "highwayman" who demands "your money or your life" and condemned democracy with the trenchant comment "a man is no less a slave because he is permitted to choose a new master once in a term of years."

Benjamin Tucker was a contemporary of Spooner's who founded and edited the anarchist periodical *Liberty*, in which he printed some of Spooner's writings, as well as those of other notable thinkers at the time and his own translations of foreign language works. In giving a platform to nonconformist writers about government, Tucker played an important role in the developing liberty movement in America.

Both Spooner and Tucker belonged to the Individualist Anarchist movement. It is important to differentiate this movement from others going under the name of anarchy, as it possessed rather different goals and philosophical underpinnings. Anarchy as a political philosophy emerged in Russia through radical writers like Emma Goldman. At that time, it was essentially a variant on Marx's proposed communist society, in which the institution of the state would "wither away" leaving everyone free to pursue their own life choices without either government or corporate oppression. It was under communism that anarchism acquired its reputation as an ideology of violence and destruction.

In America, anarchist thought was influenced by the writings of Thomas Jefferson, John Locke, and Thomas Paine rather than those of Marx and Trotsky. Whereas anarcho-communists tended to focus on the well-being of the collective, men like Tucker and Spooner saw the individual as sovereign, and attempts by the state to interfere with individual will as a violation of man's natural condition in nature. It was in the anarchist individualist tradition that Henry David Thoreau was working when he wrote *Walden,* as well as his work on civil disobedience. Thoreau was fed up with the trappings of modern life, and decided to do what the hermits and saints of old had always done: go out into the woods and live by himself. *Walden* chronicles his experiences, mental, physical, and spiritual, and is essential reading for aficionados of weirdos, misanthropes, cranks, and troublemakers.

To live out in nature, divorced from civilized society, as well as rejecting government authority was a fairly nonconformist way of life, and Thoreau's influence was profound on those who shared his outsider tendencies. The Transcendentalist movement in philosophy credits as its twin founders Thoreau and Ralph Waldo Emerson. Yet Thoreau was not without his critics. Poet John Greenleaf Whittier reacted violently to Thoreau's work, calling him "wicked" and "heathenish", while author Robert Louis Stevenson characterized him as a "skulker" whose actions were "unmanly." None of this is surprising. What is surprising is that an offshoot from Thoreau's philosophy can be found in the bizarre marriage of spiritualism and the women's independence movement.

Activism from Beyond

Spiritualism is the practice of communicating with, you guessed it, spirits. It is characterized by séances, in which the spirits of the dead are said to communicate with the living through the body of a medium. Mediums are people who claim to possess a certain degree of psychic ability, and who have channeled it into developing a maximally receptive consciousness, such that other entities can drive out the ego and make use of the medium's physical body. Because of the necessity of surrendering control of one's own mind, mediumship can be rather risky business with damage to the individual's personality being a common occupational hazard.

Spiritualism is also concerned with such phenomena as table turning, unexplained knocking, and the use of props such as the Ouija board to assist in communication. Although largely written off as nonsense and charlatanism today, for a brief time in the nineteenth century spiritualism was a booming business. It was also controversial, with author Arthur Conan Doyle being an enthusiastic supporter and stage magician Harry Houdini devoting considerable energy to exposing frauds and proving that it was nothing but a bunch of parlor tricks. No less a person than First Lady Mary Todd Lincoln invited spiritualists into the White House to perform séances. More than anything else, though, the flames of spiritualism were fanned by the high-profile case of the Fox sisters.

In 1848, Kate and Margaret Fox, aged twelve and fourteen, reported hearing mysterious rapping noises in their home in Hydesville, New York. The reports attracted the interests of their neighbors, who would visit to hear the sounds, and in time the sisters began to claim that the sounds were being made by spirits, and that they could interpret raps as answers to yes-or-no questions. The story of the Fox sisters' alleged abilities spread, being cheered on by some friends who were practicing Quakers. The Quaker religion is notable here for its doctrine that an inner divine light resides within each individual, a belief that not only gave credence to supernatural spiritual abilities like those claimed by the Fox sisters, but which also undermined to a certain extent church authority to dictate dogma from the top down.

Soon, spiritualism took on the status of a religion in its own right, enjoying nationwide success. While Thoreau and Emerson wrote in no uncertain terms about their disapproval of spiritualism, their Transcendentalist ideas of divinity in nature and individual sovereignty were immensely influential among spiritualists.

In retrospect, skepticism about the veracity of spiritualist claims seems rather beside the point. The movement was similar to a religion, yes, but more than anything else it was built around a desire for political change. It didn't take long for spiritualism's focus to shift from disembodied voices in darkened parlors to a campaign for women's equality, abolition of slavery, and individual rights. Although there were male mediums, the ability to talk with spirits was, and continues to be, overwhelmingly associated with women, probably because of the receptive and empathetic qualities required of a successful medium. In her fascinating treatment of the subject, *Radical Spirits,* author Ann Braude explains:

> *Spiritualism's greatest contribution to the crusade for woman's rights lay in the new role of spirit medium. While reformers talked about women's autonomy, mediumship cast women in a central public role in the new religion. Far from requiring guidance from men, mediums led both men and women on the path to truth. The example of mediums, whose religious role encouraged them to take charge of their own lives, reinforced the application of the principle of individual sovereignty to women. In mediumship, women's religious leadership became normative for the first time in American history.*[40]

Spiritualists embraced a radical individualism similar to that espoused by Benjamin Tucker and Lysander Spooner, called out the church for its complicity in the institution of slavery, and criticized marriage as a means of robbing women of their autonomy by shackling them to a man, often unwillingly or only out of reasons of financial necessity. The overlap here between politics, religion, and matters seen as occult is instructive in showing that nonconformists come in many varieties, and often manifest their nonconformity in multiple ways simultaneously.

Naturally, spiritualism's attack on so many cherished traditions was met with resistance. Some mediums were denounced as heretics and excommunicated for their beliefs. While stage magicians like Houdini denounced the spiritualists because they believed them to be frauds, others denounced them for exactly the opposite reason. Most were decried as charlatans and imposters.

Montague Summers, in his *History of Witchcraft and*

Demonology deals with the subject at some length. As a devoted witch-hunter writing contemporaneously with the spiritualist movement, it is unsurprising that he exhibits more than his usual level of alarm. Interestingly, he asserts that mediumship carries a severe risk of demonic possession, which the secular authorities are liable to misinterpret as mental illness. It is indeed strange to see so modern an authority ascribing the symptoms of mental illness to demonic influence rather than the other way around, but Summers was nothing if not eccentric. In his closing argument against spiritualism, he has the following to say:

> *How then are we to regard this mighty movement at which it were folly to sneer, which it is impossible to ignore? The Catholic Church does neither. But none the less she condemns it utterly and entirely. Not because she disbelieves in it, but because she believes in it so thoroughly. Because she knows what is the real nature of the moving forces, however skillfully they may disguise themselves, however quick and subtle their shifts and turns, the intelligences which inform and direct the whole. It is a painful subject since (I reiterate) many good people, no doubt many thoughtful seekers after truth have been fascinated and swept along by Spiritism. They are as yet conscious of neither physical nor moral harm, and, it may be, they have been playing with the fire for years. Nay more, Spiritism has been a sweet solace to many in most poignant hours of bitter sorrow and loss; wherefore it is hallowed in their eyes by tenderest memories. They are woefully deceived. Hard as it may seem, we must get down to the bed-rock of fact. Spiritism has been specifically condemned on no less than four occasions by the Holy Office, whose decree, 30 March, 1989, utterly forbids all Spiritistic practices although intercourse with demons be strictly excluded, and communication sought with good spirits only. Modern Spiritism is merely Witchcraft revived.*[41]

Summers here perhaps overstates the hostility of the Catholic Church to the spiritualist movement; enforcement of this prohibition through excommunication or charges of heresy did occur, but at hardly the rates common in earlier eras. Nevertheless, he is correct in citing the Church's official disapproval and suspicion of a belief system that conflicted with Catholic doctrine.

Perhaps the most telling reaction against the spiritualists were the attacks from the medical establishment on what they viewed as a threat to their profession. Accepted wisdom in medicine had long held that women were physically frail by nature, prone to disease and fainting, and that any strenuous activity would put their delicate constitutions at unacceptable risk. This assumption was used to justify keeping women out of all sorts of traditionally male professions, including medicine itself. Spiritualists encouraged women to be healers, and male doctors weren't too happy about the competition. Ann Braude writes:

Male doctors attacked women in general during this period as unfit to practice medicine, or any other profession, because of an anatomical proclivity to hysteria. The medical attack on mediums was a special case, and an especially vehement one, of the medical attack on women in general. Doctors who viewed the female organization as inherently pathological saw mediums, who exemplified so many feminine qualities, as prime examples of pathology.[42]

Neurologists and other doctors were keen to ascribe the behavior of mediums to hysteria, catalepsy, and a variety of other questionable mental disorders. These attacks represent the continuation of a pattern we saw in Chapter 6, the tendency to write off any undesirable or inconvenient behavior as a kind of madness.

Eventually, the spiritualist movement fell apart due to internal divisions and a lack of agreement over the proper way to organize. One of the problems with radical individualists is that they don't like being pigeonholed, and frequently resist opportunities for collective action. Spiritualists were no exception, with many leaders in the movement resenting the very ideas of being forced to operate within the confined structure of a formal organization. In 1888, Margaret Fox claimed that the phenomena experienced by her and her sister had been nothing more than a hoax, and although she later tried to backtrack on this claim, that was pretty much the end of the movement. Nevertheless, it's fair to say that spiritualism was responsible for gaining important ground in the fight for individual rights and women's liberation, ground which is too often overlooked by historians in favor of mocking the credulous and condemning mediums as frauds.

Embracing the Unholy

When society persists in slapping a label onto a certain class of persons, particularly when that label amounts to a hateful epithet, there are essentially two courses of action available. One can reject the label, argue that it is inaccurate or cruel, and try to build oneself up as a model of respectable normalcy in order to avoid being singled out. Or, one can embrace the label and make it one's own, taking pride in the term and thereby robbing it of its power to wound or offend. We have seen this happen in recent times with slurs directed at certain racial groups or towards people with certain sexual preferences. The pejorative terms are adopted as symbols of solidarity and fellowship, as well as resistance against oppression.

There is an element of psychological self-defense in this method. An insult will not tend to sting so badly if it's something you choose to call yourself. In a way, it's the inverse of the parable of the fox and the grapes. "I was going to call myself that anyway" is as good a retort as any to the slings and arrows of those who would taunt or bully with words.

We can see this playing out beginning in the eighteenth century with nonconformists who figured that if society insisted on calling them demonic, they might as well revel in it. Sir Francis Dashwood was a flamboyant English aristocrat who, like most English aristocrats, liked booze and sex. Unlike most of his peers, however, he decided not to conceal these vices under a cloak of shame, but instead celebrate them in the most elaborate possible style. With this intention, he founded the Hell-Fire Club in 1746 as a monument to debauchery — actually the revival of an older, short-lived secret society from a few decades before. Dashwood extravagantly renovated a medieval monastery and held wild parties there in keeping with the aesthetics of the emerging genre of Gothic literature. As John Michael Greer writes in his survey of secret societies throughout history:

> *Members dressed in black robes and took part in burlesque pseudo-Satanic rites, accompanied by scantily clad "nuns" who were either noblewomen of easy virtue or prostitutes hired for the weekend. Astonishing amounts of liquor were consumed in these celebrations, which inevitably ended with an orgy.*[43]

Of course, Dashwood and the members of the Hell-Fire club were not Satanists, nor did they worship evil. They were just ordinary bored, rich noblemen with nothing better to do with their time and enough spare cash to go around buying up old castles for the sake of a good party. But given that their particular tastes ran contrary to the accepted mores of society at the time, they found it fun and provocative to preempt criticism by pretending to be what they knew others would accuse them of. As we shall soon see, Dashwood was not the last person to take such an idea and run with it.

The Wickedest Man in the World

One of the nineteenth century's most interesting characters was a young man named Aleister Crowley. Crowley exhibited the typical boredom and rebelliousness of a kid born to wealthy parents in an atmosphere of stodgy Victorianism, but unlike most of his contemporaries, he proved to be uncommonly talented at anything he turned his hand to. He was an expert mountaineer, a prolific writer and, most famously, a brilliant occultist.

Crowley was born in 1875, and as a young man pursued a variety of activities, most with some success, before turning his attention to the occult. In 1898, he encountered Samuel Liddell MacGregor Mathers through their mutual love of spending time in antiquarian reading rooms in London libraries. Mathers, along with his friend Wynn Westcott, had discovered and translated some ancient manuscripts dealing with the subject of magic, and on that basis had founded a secret society known as The Hermetic Order of the Golden Dawn.

Borrowing heavily from the traditions of Freemasonry, Egyptian magic, Jewish mysticism, Pythagorean teachings, and a little bit of European witchcraft, the Golden Dawn quickly became the preeminent magical society in Britain. The rituals and ceremonial practices developed by the order remain the standard blueprints for modern day occultists. Even though the order's actual existence was relatively brief, its influence has been unmatched even a hundred years later.

The Golden Dawn attracted a wide range of diverse personalities, from scholars like Arthur Edward Waite, whose most famous achievement was modernizing and standardizing the system of tarot cards still in use today, to writers like Arthur Machen, a contemporary and influencer of H.P. Lovecraft, to poets like W.B. Yeats, who had a fascination with Irish folklore and fairy legends. It is unfortunate that the name "Golden Dawn" has today been appropriated by a fascist political party in Greece, an organization that is wholly unrelated to the Hermetic Order. The actual work of the Golden Dawn was largely devotional, spiritual, and related to uncovering the mysteries of the universe while training members in methods of self-knowledge, enlightenment, and union with the divine. There was no political agenda, and many of the surviving members actively fought against fascism during the Second World War.

Crowley was instantly attracted to the order, and once admitted advanced very quickly. He read voraciously, and showed a natural talent for occult thinking. He also traveled extensively, and was one of the first Europeans to make a concerted study of yoga and other Hindu and Buddhist spiritual practices.

Of course, Crowley's achievements were matched by his ego, and he quickly began to squabble with Mathers and other members, insisting that he was more capable of running the Order and that their leadership was inept and misguided. Crowley scoffed at the sparkling and evocative poetry of Yeats, declaring himself the far superior artist. Basically, Crowley was incapable of recognizing superiority in another human being. It had to be his way, or the highway.

Having failed to take over the Golden Dawn and being expelled in the process, Crowley founded a similar society called the Ordo Templi Orientis, or the O.T.O. During this time, he was engaged in systematically devising his own religion which he called Thelema. The name comes from a series of ribald satirical books by sixteenth century French writer Francois Rabelais about the giants Gargantua and Pantagruel, the former supplying the origin of the modern word "gargantuan". One of these books tells of an abbey called the Abbé Thélème, which is governed solely by the law "Do what thou wilt." Crowley modified this law for his own purposes, expanding it to "Do what thou wilt shall be the whole of the law. Love is the law, love under will."

Some have described Crowley as a cult leader, and this is not wholly without merit. He set up his own abbey for religious instruction, where he certainly took great liberties with his female students, using them for his own gratification under conditions of questionable consent. He was also famous for hosting public rituals that delighted in spectacle, and it has been said that he would surreptitiously slip hallucinogenic drugs to his audience in order to enhance their experiences. He seemed to have no great respect for others, in spite of the libertarian flavor of his supposed code of ethics.

Crowley is also frequently accused of being a Satanist by those who only know of him tangentially. And while he was many things, not all of them pleasant, Satanism was certainly not among his interests. In fact, there's nothing in his writings to indicate that he even believed in Satan or any supremely evil force. He certainly didn't worship such a being. Such subjugation would have been intolerable to his ego, although he did claim to work with a variety of immaterial spirits throughout his career. But if Crowley is unjustly accused of Satanism, it is not as if he did anything to discourage such beliefs. In fact, he reveled in public scorn, and courted controversy wherever possible.

An odd-looking fellow with a shaved head, deeply sunken eyes, and a perpetual scowl on his face, Crowley's look alone was enough to distinguish himself from his contemporaries. He was often photographed in elaborate ceremonial garb or in the robes and turbans of an Eastern mystic. Reading through the instructions for some of the Golden Dawn ceremonies conjures up pictures of elaborate temples housing dozens of participants wearing outlandish costumes and utilizing a vast array of prompts, all while chanting in often indecipherable languages like Enochian, the alleged language of the angels revealed by Queen Elizabeth's court wizard, John Dee. Crowley was also a confessed drug addict, and did little either to hide or curb his voracious appetites. His penchant for sex has already been remarked upon. In short, Crowley gloried in being the very antithesis to Victorian modesty and puritanism.

When the newspapers dubbed him "the wickedest man in the world" he gleefully adopted the epithet and used it as often as possible in describing himself. He also would occasionally refer to himself as "The Great Beast" and employ the number 666 for its shock value.

For students of the occult, Crowley continues to represent something of a paradox. His writings remain some of the most lucid and insightful ever composed on the subject, and his influence is nothing short of vast. The field would be immeasurably poorer had he not chosen to apply his peculiar talents in that particular direction. On the other hand, Crowley did little to dispel the bad reputation of occultists, cementing the idea in the public imagination that everyone with esoteric interests must therefore also engage in hedonistic, drug-fueled orgies and worship the Devil. A film like Stanley Kubrick's *Eyes Wide Shut*, while very entertaining, continues to propagate these misconceptions, drawn largely from the extravagant life of Aleister Crowley.

Though hardly an innocent, Crowley shows clearly the eagerness with which the media likes to classify weirdos and outsiders as necessarily doing the bidding of evil. I am the first to admit that Crowley must have been a fairly unpleasant person, domineering, arrogant, a bully, perhaps even a sociopath. On the other hand, it's unlikely that his actual misconduct is any worse than one might find in a close examination of generally beloved figures like John F. Kennedy or Bill Clinton. He was simply more public and unapologetic in his particular brand of hedonism. Whereas politicians strive to maintain an aura of respectability, Crowley did the exact opposite. One would be hard pressed to find a more outspoken nonconformist; the fact that his legacy remains one of confused accusations and uninformed fear should hardly be surprising.

The Artist as Individualist

Even in the absence of his occult fascinations, it is unlikely that Crowley would have been accepted as a "respectable" member of society. His appetites were too large, his opinion of himself too high, and his contempt for convention too vocal. Although not a great talent when it came to poetry or literature, he possessed that same spirit of artistic independence and integrity that we saw in Ayn Rand's fictional architect Howard Roark in an earlier chapter. Indeed, the world of art has always been one dedicated to pushing boundaries, thwarting traditions, and exalting the vision of the individual in ways not always comfortable for defenders of the status quo. The very goal of art is to create something new and different, and things which are new and different tend to be threatening to those committed to an established order.

As we have seen, the poet Milton created an archetypical antihero defined by personal pride and his unwillingness to bend the knee for anyone, including the almighty himself. Milton's Lucifer is willing to pay any price for his integrity, even being condemned to Hell for all eternity. It cannot be surprising that some artists were able to find inspiration and identification in such a figure. After all, history is littered with tales of the inspired man of genius who dies in poverty and obscurity because the world is not ready to accept his vision, his greatness only retrospectively realized through the lens of history many years afterwards. What a source of solace for the young artistic firebrand, eager to make his mark on the world but frustrated by a lack of commercial or critical success!

Contemporary analyses of Milton's Lucifer often describe the character as a "Byronic Hero". The term comes from the nineteenth century romantic poet Lord Byron, known for creating dramatic, moody, brooding, and somewhat sinister characters notable for their intensity of purpose and proud integrity. Byron's characters were often considered to be avatars for his own rebellious personality, which tended strongly towards the bucking of convention. Like Ayn Rand, Byron took the conventional sin of pride and inverted it, presenting it rather as a mark of virtue. The proud man is strong, capable, independent, intelligent, and indomitable. He represents all that is great about the human spirit. He will not humiliate himself or permit others to humiliate him. Most importantly, he has something to be proud *of*. The meek may inherent the Earth, but for the present they are condemned to lives free from conviction, satisfaction, accomplishment, or self-respect, and that, according to Byron, is no way to live.

Byron wrote a number of influential works of poetry espousing these views, and for which he was predictably condemned. An English clergyman called Reginald Heber accused Byron of "devoting himself and his genius to the adornment and extension of evil." A fellow poet, Robert Southey, suggested that the movement in poetry represented by Byron should be called The Satanic School, because his writing was "characterized by a Satanic spirit of pride and audacious impiety." With Byron, Southey lumped in the poet Percy Blythe Shelley, a somewhat militant atheist who condemned the Judeo-Christian God as a tyrannical figure before whom he refused to prostrate himself. Shelley's writing, though less controversial than Byron's, shared a spirit of relentless independence, individualism, and artistic integrity that shocked more conservative and pious critics. It is here worth noting that Shelley's wife, Mary Shelley, was the author of Frankenstein, to which she gave the alternate title "A Modern Prometheus." The significance of Prometheus to nonconformists will be recalled from Chapter 1, and although Victor Frankenstein can hardly be considered a heroic figure in the book, the battle of wills between the iconoclastic scientist and his creation stands as a veritable clash of the Titans in literary history, displaying all the characteristic features of the Byronic worldview.

Unlike some other artists, whom we will examine in a moment, Byron and Shelley were not called Satanic because they were believed to *worship* Satan. As Reginald Heber later clarified, he did not believe that Byron *worshipped* anything, and indeed, that was the problem. It was a personal identification with Satan, a rebellion against authority and a refusal to accept a power higher and more noble than man himself that critics like Southey considered so dangerous and unholy.

Musicianship and Other Demonic Talents

The legend of Faust is one of the most famous and commonly retold stories in the western world. Originally a German folk tale, the story was famously dramatized by the poet Johann Wolfgang von Goethe, as well as by the playwright Christopher Marlowe. The plot varies from version to version, but the key points remain the same. A highly educated scholar named Faust becomes frustrated at the limitations of his own understanding of the universe, and in exchange for vast knowledge, including the hidden occult powers of magicians and alchemists, he makes a deal with a demon called Mephistopheles — a clear analog for the Devil himself.

Mephistopheles grants Faust's request, asking only for his immortal soul in return, and the results are predictable. Faust has a good time enjoying the fruits of his newfound knowledge — for a while. Eventually, however, he realizes the terrible mistake he has made and that his greed for worldly things will damn him for all eternity. In Marlowe's version, he ends up in Hell. In Goethe's he is redeemed by the love of a beautiful woman. But the ending is less important than the key idea of exchanging salvation for improbable earthly talents, which has endured with a vengeance.

The story of Faust has been made into movies, plays, operas, and works of instrumental music, but the "sell your soul to the Devil" motif has been even more widespread, as in the aforementioned *Twilight Zone* episode and countless other stories. As fiction, these tales are harmless enough, but the core idea has so gripped the popular imagination that it has spilled over into the real-life demonization of people with seemingly uncanny talents.

Again, this idea can be traced back to Bible at least. A little remembered story in the New Testament tells of Simon Magus, a local would-be wizard who approaches the apostle Peter in an effort to purchase occult knowledge from him. Peter rebukes Simon, claiming that such power comes only from God, and that it cannot be bought by the insincere and faithless. Undeterred, Simon undertakes his own studies in the magic arts and eventually learns how to fly. When Peter sees him hovering several stories above the ground, he is outraged and immediately falls to his knees in prayer, asking God to punish the showoff. God complies and Simon falls to his death. It seems a harsh punishment for the crime of developing talents beyond those of ordinary men, but Simon would not be the last to be treated so shabbily. From this story, we get the word "simony", which refers to the sin of attempting to buy divine favor with worldly riches.

As the story of Simon Magus illustrates, nonconformity does not only encompass the bizarre, the deviant, and the socially unacceptable. It can also be found in individuals who excel beyond the expectations or understanding of their peers, thereby inciting envy and resentment.

Strangely, this phenomenon seems to pop up in music a lot. Music has the power to soothe, to cheer, to bring people together in fellowship and cooperation, and to exalt God. It seems unlikely that an art form of such majesty and glory would be the subject of the Devil's infernal machinations. On the other hand, perhaps this attitude is not so surprising. Music has always been regarded as containing a certain element of magic. It has the power to act on the emotions, bringing about tears as easily as laughter and able to be as chilling as it is joyful. To the untrained, the ability of the musician to conjure up wonderful melodies and harmonies from a few strings of wire or a length of pipe must seem as mysterious as any conjurer's trick. It is no accident that religious ceremonies, as well as magical rituals, have featured music, singing, and chanting, for as far back as we have records.

In Greek mythology, the master musician Orpheus is forced to descend into the underworld to retrieve Euridice, his bride, from Hades, perhaps establishing an association between Hell and musicality. Pythagoras, the Greek polymath famed for his theorem about triangles, was one of the first to study music in depth, and created one of the earliest tuning systems. Pythagoras was also something of a mystic, and his theories have been carried forward by the Neoplatonists and the Rosicrucians, frequently in the form of secret societies in the western esoteric tradition. In Medieval church music, the dissonant interval of an augmented fourth was forbidden as "the Devil's interval", and early brass instruments were viewed with suspicion, their coarse sound regarded as inappropriate for divine worship.

In the country music classic, *The Devil Went Down to* Georgia, Satan is represented as an expert violinist, challenging locals to musical duels, the stakes of which were eternal damnation. Clearly, there is something inherent in musical sounds that arouses the same feelings of awe with which early humans regarded the supernatural. It therefore makes sense that the legend of Faust, in which salvation is traded for preternatural skill and knowledge, should find its extension in the world of musical performance.

In the early nineteenth century, the Italian violinist Niccolò Paganini was a victim, or one might argue a beneficiary of the tendency of audiences to ascribe supernatural origin to extraordinary technical ability. A virtuoso from a young age, Paganini mastered the mandolin and the guitar with ease, but where his ability really shone was on the violin. Partially due to technical innovations in bow construction, and partially due to his own genius, Paganini was soon astonishing audiences with technical feats once thought impossible. Even today, his *24 Caprices* for solo violin remain the gold standard for any aspiring virtuoso.

In concerts, Paganini would dazzle the audience with flamboyant displays of skill, at times snapping three of the strings on his instrument only to finish the concert on the single remaining string. Rumors began to circulate about the source of his unbelievable ability, and some began to speculate that the young man must have struck a deal with the Devil, a Faustian bargain, in order to be able to play so magnificently. These rumors were encouraged by the fact that Paganini did not exactly lead a chaste and Christian lifestyle. He drank, gambled, and womanized heavily, as one would expect from a diabolist. The resulting syphilis he contracted gave him a gaunt, skeletal appearance that enhanced the effect on stage.

It's probably no coincidence that all this happened at a time when European society began to court a fascination with all things supernatural, and music was certainly not immune to the fad. In Germany, Felix Mendelssohn wrote sprightly pieces inspired by elves and fairies. In France, Hector Berlioz included a movement in his first symphony inspired by the witches' sabbath, and Camille Saint-Saens wrote the famous *Danse Macabre*, a skeletal dance of death for orchestra. In Vienna, Hungarian composer and piano virtuoso Franz Liszt, himself hugely inspired by Paganini, composed the *Totentanz*, a monumentally diabolic theme and variations (based on the same Gregorian Chant motif that appears in Berlioz's work), that would tax even the finest pianist to his limits. The fact that Liszt himself managed to avoid charges of Satanic pacts, given his total mastery of his instrument, is remarkable, and probably due to his lifelong devotion to the Catholic Church, by which he was granted formal religious orders late in life. Paganini, on the other hand, was denied a Catholic burial by the Church at the time of his death, in part due to his alleged association with the powers of darkness.

A little over a hundred years later, the blues guitarist Robert Johnson would attract similar accusations of diabolism. Johnson, like Paganini before him, was an extraordinary musician who would go on to be a major influence on many of rock's most celebrated guitarists, including Jimmy Page and Eric Clapton. He wasn't always a star, however. Born in humble circumstances in Mississippi, Johnson's enduring desire to be a famous blues musician was reportedly greater than his talent. Upon first hearing him play, the already established blues musician Son House described his playing as extremely poor. Determined to improve, Johnson left his hometown to study his technique and by the time he came back, he had acquired an astonishing virtuosity. Amazed by this transformation, people began to circulate rumors that Johnson had met up with the devil at a crossroads late at night, where he traded his soul for the ability to play guitar. These rumors were no doubt encouraged by the fact that one of his teachers, Ike Zimmerman, was also said to have acquired his talent from visiting graveyards after dark. It is also possible that the rumors arose due to a confusion surrounding a local metaphor, in which abandoning sacred music to play secular songs was referred to as selling one's soul to the devil.

In any case, it seems that audiences as a whole had difficulty in believing that such extreme skill could be acquired through natural or wholesome means. Only the Devil, they argued, could allow someone to be that good at anything. If you stand out far enough ahead of the pack, you risk attack just as much as those falling behind or drifting off to the side. Where excellence should be celebrated, it is too often envied and despised as somehow unholy.

Johnson's legacy as a somewhat dark and sinister figure intensified after the mysterious circumstances of his death. His body was simply found by the side of the road one day, and no formal cause of death has ever been identified. Musical folklore, however, has offered the following persistently popular explanation: While playing in a bar one night, Johnson was warned against flirting with a married woman. Unwilling to listen to good sense, Johnson persisted in his affections, until he attracted the attention of a jealous husband. A slug of strychnine slipped into a glass of whiskey ensured that Johnson had sung his last song. He was 27 years old at the time, kicking off the popular theory of the "27 Club" in which great musicians like Jimmy Hendrix, Janis Joplin, Jim Morrison, Kurt Cobain, and Amy Winehouse are doomed to perish at the same ill-fated age.

As we will see in the next chapter, music continues to have a powerful impact on the emotions of listeners, and continues to draw criticism for being too different from the mainstream.

The Birth of Satanism

While the arts remained a popular target for accusations of diabolism, it was only a matter of time before the Byronic worldview began to migrate out of the artistic world and into the world of philosophy. Two of the most well-known and infamous champions of Byronic heroes and their pride-as-virtue ethical systems were Friedrich Nietzsche and the aforementioned Ayn Rand. Nietzsche was a German philosopher who famously and controversially stated that "God is dead" and pondered the implications of an atheistic universe on morality. Like Byron, he was enamored with the nobility of man himself, stressing individual action, strength, independence, and integrity as necessary components of leading a worthwhile life.

Ayn Rand was a novelist who eventually founded a

philosophical movement which she called Objectivism. Having escaped from the Soviet Union early in life, Rand was horrified by the society created by the collectivist theories of Marx and Lenin, and responded by wholeheartedly championing free markets, individual sovereignty, self-interest, and art as an inviolable expression of man's creative spirit. In her wildly popular novels like *Atlas Shrugged* and *The Fountainhead*, Rand paints pictures of uncompromising characters of supreme competence, standing alone against a world too stupid and petty to understand them. The villains in Rand's stories are obstructive bureaucrats who resent anyone with more ability than themselves, and use altruism as an excuse to destroy that which they cannot match. Rand's Objectivist philosophy builds on these same ideas, condemning those who would sacrifice their own lives and happiness out of a sense of guilt or obligation to the demands of a vague, collectivist mob. Needless to say, she remains a controversial figure, beloved by libertarians who find inspiration in her championing of the individual and condemnation of big government, and hated by pretty much everyone else.

Although Rand didn't admit any influence from the earlier Nietzsche (Aristotle was her philosopher of choice) their philosophies had enough in common that they influenced the same phenomena, namely a horrified condemnation from collectivists and Christians alike, and the eventual formation of the Church of Satan.

Anton LaVey was a talented keyboard player and church organist who grew disillusioned with Christianity and its teachings. Not being a great fan of subtlety or tact, he penned the iconoclastic *Satanic Bible* and concurrently founded the Church of Satan, the first modern institution to pay direct homage to the prince of darkness. LaVey, more than any other single individual, has done more to spread confusion and misinformation about Satanism and devil worship since the Inquisition. By calling his organization the Church of Satan, he immediately conjured up images of ritual sacrifice, rape, murder, and all sorts of unpleasantness, striking fear into the hearts of god-fearing people everywhere, and instantly ensuring unthinking condemnation for himself and anyone who happened to subscribe to his ideas.

In fact, *The Satanic Bible* is not what you think it is. First of all, it's not very Satanic, and second, it's not really a Bible. It would be more accurate to describe it as an outline of LaVey's personal philosophy, nine tenths of which is a criticism and rejection of Christian dogma. LaVey was basically a materialist who rejected mysticism and the supernatural in favor of an atheistic, libertine approach to life. If this world is all that we have, he reasoned, why not enjoy it for the short time that we exist upon its surface? He therefore advocated personal liberty, and the fullest enjoyment of all the pleasures life has to offer, including sex, food, and the comfort of a good sleep-in. Curiously, he opposed drug use, presumably because becoming addicted to anything would interfere with personal autonomy. No better to be a slave to heroin than to be a slave to an omnipotent god.

LaVey drew his inspiration from philosophers such as Nietzsche, who argued that abstract concepts of good and evil were human inventions, and Ayn Rand, who condemned sacrificing oneself for some imagined collective good, and sternly opposed religion as irrational. These ideologies can certainly be criticized on their merits, but it would be disingenuous to describe any of them as immoral or championing evil. In fact, *The Satanic Bible* explicitly condemns most actions commonly associated with diabolism. The reader is instructed to be kind to children and animals, to respect those who treat you with respect, and to ensure consent before engaging in sexual activity.

While the second half of *The Satanic Bible* does contain a decent helping of the rituals and rites you might expect from such a book, it is difficult to believe that LaVey himself took these seriously. His brief fascination with Aleister Crowley (from whom most of the ritual structure is derived) was to end due to LaVey's disgust for mysticism in general, and he certainly held no belief in a supernatural being called Satan. In all likelihood, these rituals only exist as a form of symbolic pageantry designed to simultaneously mock religious rites, to provide some sort of iconography for LaVey's followers, and for pure shock value.

If LaVey's desire was to inspire shock, fear, and anger in service of his ideas, he certainly succeeded. To this day, most people don't know the difference between someone who actually worships a deity called Satan (very rare, if not entirely fictional) and a LaVeyan Satanist acting out in rebellion against Christianity, but with no commitment to evil whatsoever.

For good or ill, LaVey's influence continues to be felt. The Church of Satan has survived the death of its founder and continues to attract sympathetic adherents today. Meanwhile, other groups have also embraced the name Satan in an effort to make themselves heard, and as a symbolic rebuke of the status quo.

For example, the Temple of Satan, which has no formal ties to the Church of Satan, exists largely as a political activism organization dedicated to the separation of church and state. Every few years, there is generally a news story about Satanists demanding a statue of Lucifer be erected outside of a courthouse or other government building. Chances are, the group in question is the Temple of Satan. Like LaVeyans, they do not believe in the literal devil, nor do they wish to do anyone any harm. They are merely protesting what they perceive as the church's intrusion into the public sphere. If Judaism or Christianity have the right to place the Ten Commandments, a thoroughly religious symbol, outside of government buildings, why then should Satanists not have the same privilege?

The recent documentary *Hail Satan?* shines a much-needed light onto the Temple and its goals, revealing not a monstrous cult, but a group of sincere misfits with fairly modest goals. The film even highlights how they were forced to expel a high-ranking member after she made an incendiary speech threatening violence against the President of the United States.

When asked why they call themselves Satanists rather than just atheists, several members explained that atheism is boring, a position defined by what it is not with no history, no iconography, and nothing that really binds adherents together. As Satanists, they get to dress up in robes, wear horned masks and pentagram necklaces — for fun. It helps them feel like more of a community with shared ideals, rather than just a group of nonbelievers.

The name also helps them get media coverage when a similarly sized group of self-styled atheists would most likely be ignored. Whether or not this media coverage is counterproductive is debatable, but the important point is the extent to which individualists with unpopular opinions are willing to embrace the pejorative label hurled at their predecessors, converting it from a damning slur into a term of personal empowerment. Of course, this approach also has its downsides. The use of Satanist terminology and iconography means that, for many people, it's impossible to distinguish between a provocative political movement dedicated to personal freedom, and the kind of barbaric, Sabbat-attending, goat sacrificing, child molesting, serial killing cult that most people imagine when they think of Satanism.

Chapter 8

The Satanic Panic

In the late 1970s and early 1980s, a number of news reports began to surface detailing horrific and gruesome crimes committed by Satanic cults. Allegations of child abuse, rape, and murder began to swirl around as the media conjured up images of black robed figures engaging in animal sacrifice in graveyards and hidden temples. The pentagram, the five-pointed star that remains one of the oldest and most revered religious symbols, emerged as an emblem of evil and violence, striking fear into the hearts of any who beheld it. The music industry was outed as being run by a cabal of Satanists eager to corrupt the youth with their unholy worldview, and new fantasy games marketed at kids were seen as the "gateway drug" for dabbling in the occult, itself a surefire path towards Satanism and a life of violent crime. Children out enjoying the harmless Halloween pastime of trick or treating were warned that their neighbors would try to harm them by secreting razor blades and rat poison into apparently tasty treats. The nation was shocked. It seemed that overnight America had transformed from a wholesome place to one which harbored sadistic and demented criminals dedicated to serving the forces of darkness, at the expense of our very safety and peace of mind. How did this happen?

The short answer is, it didn't. Almost every claim made in the above paragraph turned out to be either a hoax, an urban legend, or an outright lie cooked up by the media and bolstered by a public eager to gorge on fuel for their own paranoid fantasies. In hindsight, the freak out over Satanism during this period has been dubbed The Satanic Panic, with the word "panic" being anything but an exaggeration. This wasn't the idle worrying of a few concerned parents. Congress got involved, and innocent people were convicted of criminal offenses and sent to prison. A generation of children were subjected to traumatizing horror stories with no basis in reality. The parallels with the Salem witch trials some three hundred years earlier are obvious. Looking back, the whole phenomenon seems bizarre, but it's clear that a large part of the panic was driven by the emergence of new subcultures that refused to conform to the way things had been done until that time, and the inherent fear that such change inspires in the reactionary status quo. In this chapter, we will look at some of the specific areas of society affected by the Satanic Panic, and the effect of mass hysteria on the parties involved.

America Fails Its Intelligence Check

In 1974, a young game developer named Gary Gygax released the first edition of his tabletop roleplaying game, Dungeons and Dragons. Inspired by the success of fantasy series like J.R.R. Tolkien's *The Lord of the Rings* and Robert E. Howard's *Conan the Barbarian* stories, Gygax wanted to offer players the chance to create their own immersive fantasy world in which they could have the same sorts of adventures as their literary heroes. Armed with only a pen, paper, and some dice, players could take on the role of a noble paladin, a powerful wizard, a crafty rogue, or a strapping warrior, rescuing damsels in distress, slaying dragons, and uncovering hoards of gold and jewels. It was also a good way for shy, introverted kids who were no good at sports to socialize with like-minded friends a couple of times a week.

It took a little while for the game to catch on, but when it did, it caught on in a big way. Not only was the game fun and different from anything that had come before, its simplicity made it incredibly easy to play in almost any situation. Soccer is the world's most popular sport because you don't need any expensive or specialized equipment to play it. As long as you have a ball, a field, and some willing players, a game can always be organized. Dungeons and Dragons benefitted from a similar accessibility. It could accommodate any number of players with only the most basic props augmented by the players' imaginations.

As the popularity of the game increased, so did concern over its wholesomeness. Like most fantasy fiction, the game featured magic spells and demonic-looking monsters, which drew the objection of some Christian groups, just as the *Harry Potter* novels have attracted criticism for their alleged promotion of "witchcraft" in more recent years. The accusations against Dungeons and Dragons and its players, however, soon grew far more serious than anything Harry Potter fans had to deal with.

In 1979, a college student named James Dallas Egbert III wrote a suicide note and disappeared into his university's storm tunnels. Egbert had previously struggled with homosexuality, depression, and drug addiction, and was by all accounts not a mentally healthy individual. When his parents hired a private investigator to search for him, the detective offered the unsupported theory that Egbert's problems were the result of his involvement with Dungeons and Dragons. The media seized upon this narrative, and the idea that Egbert had lost the ability to separate fantasy from reality, and was using the steam tunnels to "act out" his fantasy adventures became commonplace.

Egbert's suicide attempt was unsuccessful and he was eventually found, but a year later he succeeded in killing himself with a gunshot wound to the head. His story, complete with exaggerated claims that the roleplaying game caused Egbert to have a psychotic breakdown, was fictionalized in the 1981 novel *Mazes and Monsters*, which was later adapted into a made-for-television film starring Tom Hanks in 1982.

Dungeons and Dragons also features in one of the notorious "Chick Tract" comics that you may have been unfortunate enough to receive on Halloween as a child in lieu of candy. Jack

T. Chick was a fundamentalist Christian cartoonist whose Chick Publications produced and distributed dozens of cautionary comics warning against the modern world's innumerable threats to piety and salvation. These threats are largely represented as "other religions" including paganism, Judaism, Islam, and Catholicism. In Chick's tract *Dark Dungeons*, he represents role playing games as tools for initiating unsuspecting youngsters into evil witch covens, and suggests that these games can lead to suicide, playing into the Egbert story and media-created stereotypes.

In 1996, an improvisational comedy troupe known as The Dead Alewives released an audio sketch poking fun at the panic surrounding Dungeons and Dragons. In the preamble, a stern voice warns of the sinister occult peril that awaits anyone who dares to play the game. The rest of the sketch involves a handful of socially awkward teenagers realistically playing the game by arguing over the rules, searching for snacks in the next room, and lusting after imaginary wenches. It's a humorous observation that the people who criticize tabletop roleplaying games have very obviously never actually played one.

The fear surrounding Dungeons and Dragons stems from ignorance of the game and a lack of understanding of its appeal. Kids who get into role playing are generally introverted, intellectual, bookish, and imaginative. By failing to conform to the expectation of outdoor play, athletics, and popularity, these individuals tend to inspire a suspicion that something must be "wrong" with them which, coupled with fundamentalist views about magic and fantasy, lead some to associate roleplaying with Satanism, rather than its natural antecedents of improvisational theatre and communal storytelling.

The legacy of the Dungeons and Dragons controversy still crops up on occasion with respect to other, similar games. In 1993, the wildly popular *Magic: The Gathering* collectible card game was introduced, featuring evocative artwork and world building deeply rooted in the traditional fantasy genre, as developed by J.R.R. Tolkien and, yes, Dungeons and Dragons. The game, still popular today, features five colors of magic available to the player, each color emphasizing a different elemental or moral quality. For example, red cards deal with fire magic, green with nature magic, and white cards focus on protection. Of course, the black cards have obvious associations with necromancy and the demonic.

Magic: The Gathering managed to exist without controversy for two years, before the moral guardians got wind of it. Facing criticism for the alleged promotion of evil sorcery, and eager to avoid the reputational damage that Dungeons and Dragons faced, Wizards of the Coast, the makers of the game responded by removing cards with the word "demon" in the title, and by airbrushing out a pentagram from the illustration of the card *Unholy Strength*. Explaining the decision in a 2004 article, head designer Mark Rosewater writes:

> So why did demons go away in Magic? Because it seemed like a safe choice in a very unsafe time. Magic was on the cusp of becoming a highly public game. Wizards knew what had happened to D&D when it went through that phase.[44]

This is a great example of how the past condemnations do not simply go away when public pressure is lifted. People remember what happened to others, and wish to avoid the same fate for themselves. The result is an enduring chilling effect on freedom of expression that can't really be measured, but which nevertheless exists, continuing to damage the individual's ability to stand out from the crowd for decades after an initial incident.

Heavy Metal Madness
Fantasy role playing game enthusiasts were not the only

subculture targeted by the Satanic Panic. A major source of controversy surrounded the new sorts of music that were emerging in the late seventies and early eighties, specifically heavy metal and goth music.

Heavy metal actually started almost a decade earlier as a form of amplified blues that got gradually darker with time. Some people credit Led Zeppelin with inventing the genre, while others point to extremely loud blues bands like Blue Cheer, or even individual tracks like The Beatles' *Helter Skelter*. While the blurry lines between musical genres are mostly a matter of opinion, these people are wrong. Heavy metal was invented in 1970 with the release of the self-titled debut album of a band from Birmingham, England. That band was called Black Sabbath.

Originally gigging around the local pubs playing a similar kind of amped up blues rock to their contemporaries, the band, then called Earth, discovered that they got more attention when they darkened their sound and coupled it with lyrics about witches and death. The guitarist, Tony Iommi, had suffered an accident in which the tips of several of his fingers had been sliced off. In order to make it bearable to play his instrument, he loosened the strings, resulting in a darker, lower-pitched sound that would soon become iconic. Iommi's gift for coming up with catchy riffs combined with front man Ozzy Osbourne's eerie, high pitched wail and onstage antics were a recipe for immediate success, as well as controversy.

The band changed their name to the appropriately sinister Black Sabbath after the title of a B-horror movie, and released their first album. While most of the music is still fairly tame and bluesy, the title track features the sounds of rain, church bells, and a riff built around the "devil's interval", a dissonant sound once forbidden in church music due to its association with the forces of darkness. The lyrics concern a man terrified for his soul after coming face to face with a witch, and features Ozzy screaming "God help me!" and other ominous lines. It was a game changer that immediately spawned countless imitators, and a new genre was born.

Throughout the rest of the seventies, Sabbath's music continued to evolve and develop. While always heavy, it was not nearly as Satanic or even as dark as people imagine. The occasional reference to demons and wizards is generally eclipsed by dozens of songs about those traditional rock staples of sex, drugs, and, well, rock itself. Some of their songs even have downright Christian themes in them. *After Forever,* from their third album *Master of Reality,* warns about the dangers of atheism and admonishes listeners to worship God if they want to be saved. Never the type to get hung up on details, the moral guardians did not let this deter them from singling out heavy metal music as the latest form of seduction of the innocent.

Less talented bands recognized that they could get attention by aping Black Sabbath's aesthetic, and taking it to new extremes, and so the 80s saw a rash of album covers with depictions of pentagrams, upside down crosses, and symbolism from ritual magic and occult secret societies. Ozzy Osbourne's second solo album, *Diary of a Madman,* features writing in the Theban alphabet, a cipher used in some occult circles. Of course, the singer himself knew little or nothing about any of this. The writing had been selected from a magazine by the sleeve designer, probably because it looked cool, and when translated said nothing more sinister than "The Ozzy Osbourne Band."

There are few topics as widely misunderstood and as peppered with misinformation as that of occult symbolism, particularly as applied to rock music. The vast majority of the time, when the moral guardians get upset about the use of a particular symbol, they have no idea what it actually represents. Ill-informed guesses become accepted dogma, without ever bothering to consult those who use such symbols in earnest as to their meanings.

A prime example of this is the so-called "devil horns" hand sign displayed by some heavy metal concert goers. Josh McDowell and Don Stewart demonstrate this error in their book *The Occult: The Authority of the Believer Over the Powers of Darkness*, a typical fundamentalist screed against secular culture in general.

The satanic hand sign with the index finger and little finger extended from a closed hand is seen at nearly every rock concert and on album covers since the days of the Beatles' Yellow Submarine *album.*[45]

Almost nothing in this sentence is true. The hand sign in question is not now, nor has it ever been, satanic. Ironically, it is quite the opposite. The gesture is an old Italian blessing intended to ward off curses or "the evil eye." Known as the *mano cornuta*, the horned hand, it is a traditional gesture most popularly known in Naples.

As a potent gesture protecting against the evil eye, the mano cornuta *is constant and persistent. A Neapolitan's right hand is almost constantly in that position, pointing downwards, just as the hand charms are made to hang downwards, and in this position they take the place of an amulet worn habitually against unknown and unexpected attacks.*[46]

Catholics have been employing the gesture for centuries, but its use in rock music can be traced to singer Ronnie James Dio, a powerful vocalist who spent his early career bouncing around from band to band, fronting such hard rock and heavy metal bands as Elf, Rainbow, and eventually his own group called simply Dio. He also spent a couple of albums taking over lead vocal duties in Black Sabbath after Ozzy Osbourne was fired from the band for his unprofessionalism. Unlike Ozzy, however,

Dio didn't go around biting the heads off bats or draping himself in occult regalia. His lyrics tended to be more positive, as seen in his early hits *Holy Diver* and *Rainbow in the Dark*. One of the songs on his first solo album, *Don't Talk to Strangers*, celebrates individuality and experience, critiquing those who let fear deter them from all the best things life has to offer, but it would be difficult to find anything resembling Satanism in any of his work.

Dio, as you might have guessed from his name, came from an Italian Catholic family, and when he witnessed his grandmother making the traditional hand sign to ward off evil, he thought it looked cool. He started using it in concerts, and it caught on with fans. That's all there is to the story. No sinister conspiracy or covert efforts at indoctrination, just an Italian blessing that some ambitious journalist chose to misinterpret in order to shock readers. It's also worth noting that Dio's popularity postdates the release of *Yellow Submarine* by nearly a decade. An examination of the album cover reveals that John Lennon does appear to be making the sign, and there are also photos from around the same time of him employing the same gesture. This is likely something he learned when studying in India, as the gesture is also used in some varieties of Hinduism and Buddhism with a similar protective sense. Dio never references John Lennon when talking about his use of the sign, and it is likely that the similar use is nothing more than coincidence. In any case, no tradition, whether Buddhist, Hindu, or Catholic uses the 'horns" sign as any form of devil worship.

No symbol has been more grossly abused and profoundly misunderstood by the popular press than the pentagram, or five-pointed star. Again, this is a very ancient symbol with a variety of meanings, none of which is anything like an endorsement of Satanism. In neopagan religions, the pentagram generally represents the classical elements. Each of the four lower points corresponds to the force of Air, Fire, Earth, and Water, with the uppermost point representing the human spirit. In a sense, it is a symbol of universalism and unity with the natural world. Like the horns, it has also been used for protection, and is sometimes inscribed within circles during ceremonies to mark a sacred space or protect the operators from outside influence. Another interpretation has the pentagram correspond to the human body, its points echoing our anatomy of four limbs and a head. Superimposing a pentagram on Leonardo Da Vinci's famous drawing of Vitruvian Man, for example, reveals how well the symbol matches our proportions.

In fairness to its critics, it is true that modern Satanists have adopted the pentagram, inverted with two points up and one down, as a symbol, but this is no knock on the pentagram itself. Satanists also use an inverted Calvary cross, but that use does not taint the cross itself with Satanic associations any more than the misuse of the pentagram renders that symbol demonic. Even the inverted pentagram, notwithstanding its modern associations, is not an inherently Satanic symbol. In its traditional use as a symbol of the elements, the two-points-up position is simply another way of looking at the world, with nature on top and the spirit below. This is sometimes used to differentiate "high magic" with its focus on ceremony and human will, from "low magic" which recognizes and makes use of the sacred properties of the natural world.

It's doubtful that rock musicians or the designers of album covers know very much about these matters. Like most commercial art, I suspect that most of these designs had more to do with looking cool than with promoting a particular ideology or message. But even the ones who deliberately set out to use offensive and shocking symbolism are not generally acting on behalf of some evil deity. Few if any of these bands actually practiced anything close to Satanism. They were just using shock value and interesting visuals to sell records. So, what else is new? They probably had no idea how seriously their childish antics would be taken.

In 1985, a young man named James Vance attempted suicide and failed. He then tried to sue the heavy metal band Judas Priest, claiming that their music contained subliminal messages that encouraged him to take his own life. Ultimately, the band was not held liable for the attempted suicide, but the suggestion that subliminal messages in music could surreptitiously spread evil was one that quickly caught hold of the American imagination. The practice of backmasking, where words or sounds were recorded backwards onto a record had been in occasional use for years. The Beatles experimented heavily with the technique, giving rise to rumors about Paul McCartney's death and replacement with a lookalike. With the fear of Satanism and this new style of sinister music gaining popularity, religious crusaders set about playing every record they could get ahold of backwards, looking for secret coded messages.

Of course, if you look hard enough for something, you're going to find it, even if it doesn't exist. The human mind is incredibly good at finding patterns in largely random stimuli. It's why we see animals in clouds and faces in woodgrain, and why psychiatrists sometimes use the Rorschach "inkblot" test to get insight into how a person's mind works. If you listen to backwards music, you will mostly just hear meaningless noise, but listen long enough, with a specific goal in mind, and sooner or later you will start to be able to pick out intelligible voices. The most famous example of unintentional backmasking comes from Led Zeppelin's iconic song *Stairway to Heaven*. The song lyrics when played forward consist largely of the kind of Tolkien-inspired fantasy that was popular in the late sixties, harmless enough stuff. But when played backwards, a certain phrase sounds like "Here's to my sweet Satan." That is, *kind of* sounds like it, if you are told that you should expect to hear that phrase beforehand. The phrase isn't really there, it's just a psychological trick. But the fact that Led Zeppelin made heavy music that the kids liked, and that the particular album from which *Stairway to Heaven* comes features four undecipherable, mystical-looking symbols as its title, was enough to convince many people that the band was up to no good. If you take the time to look, you can find lists of dozens of these allegedly backmasked Satanic messages collected by zealots. And if you listen to the audio clips yourself, you can easily see how far these people had to reach in order to discover evil lurking in their children's vinyl collection.

After the James Vance lawsuit, it became common practice to examine the record collection of any teenage criminal, suicide, or troublemaker of any kind. Because teenagers tended to like the new music that was popular at the time, it was not hard to find copies of albums by Black Sabbath, Motorhead, Judas Priest, Blue Öyster Cult, or Alice Cooper lying around, and to therefore make the logical leap that the music itself must have had something to do with the crimes. We see the same pattern today when the 24-hour news media digs through the bookshelf of a school shooter to look for clues as to the "why?" of an otherwise senseless tragedy. If they find a Koran, they can attribute the shooting to radical Islamic terrorism. If they find an Ann Coulter book, they can attribute to hateful right-wing xenophobia. If they find *The Communist Manifesto*, they can blame the ideas of Karl Marx. I can only imagine what these amateur detectives would make of my own library, which includes not only Ayn Rand and Karl Marx, but also the Bible, lots of books on anarchy, and about a hundred volumes on occultism.

A big part of the reason why heavy metal was singled out as the Devil's music has to do, no doubt, with the way the musicians, and to an even greater extent the fans, looked and dressed. Leather jackets, metal chains, outlandish hairdos, tattoos, and lots and lots of black. They looked different from what society expected of music lovers, and just as Elvis was condemned for his gyrating hips and the Beatles lambasted for their shaggy hair, metal heads were equally reviled, as well as feared. All this has a certain irony, as anyone who actually listens to the lyrics of heavy metal music will realize that the fans are anything from threatening. Like the Dungeons and Dragons crowd, these kids were mostly lonely, social outcasts interested in wizards, robots, spaceships, elves, the heroes of Greek, Roman, and Norse mythology. In short, they were nerds, nerds who paradoxically found that putting on makeup and dressing funny could make them seem intimidating, rather than simply the target of after-school bullying.

Oh My Goth

We would be remiss in talking about 1980s subculture driven by loners and misfits wearing black without mentioning the Goth movement. Although still active today, albeit somewhat diluted by the Hot Topic-ization of the aesthetic, Goths were less aggressive than metal heads, defined instead by their soulful, melancholy demeanor and penchant for black clothing and white makeup. Goths get their name from the Gothic movement in literature, beginning in the eighteenth century and emphasizing the darker side of human emotion with a supernatural twist, generally set in moldering old castles and (you guessed it) Gothic cathedrals.

Goth music has some overlap with metal, but it's generally softer, slower, more romantic, and more reliant on keyboards than guitars. The primary distinguishing feature is gloomy vocals and the overall look of the band. Black eyeliner goes a long way to securing one's Goth credentials, which is how Robert Smith of the Cure, one of Goth's biggest and most influential bands, got away with writing the relentlessly cheerful single *Friday, I'm in Love.*

Were Goths subjected to the same level of fear and legal scrutiny as metal heads? Not generally, but they were certainly viewed with suspicion. Perhaps due to their smaller numbers and correspondingly weaker sphere of influence, the FBI never spent much time investigating the Goth fad. Still, it was generally assumed that teenagers who insisted on dour androgyny and black nail polish must be up to at least some kind of Satanic mischief. At the very least, mental health issues were assumed. After all, "normal" kids were supposed to be cheerful, athletic, and blonde. Failing to fit in with the stereotype made loners even lonelier. The Goth community gave them a way to find companionship and like-minded friends who would not judge them for failing to conform to the expectations of their parents and teachers.

Urban Legends and Imaginary Cults

The Satanic Panic had a far broader and more serious impact than frivolous lawsuits against rock bands and overreactions to role playing games. At its peak, the movement did some very real damage to innocent people, a literal witch-hunt in which paranoia and superstition overcame logic and sound legal judgment to devastating effect.

In 1980, psychiatrist Lawrence Pazder published a book entitled *Michelle Remembers*, coauthored by the titular Michelle, a long-term patient of his. The book, presented as non-fiction, recounts Pazder's experiences with Michelle, whom he had treated for depression and a variety of other psychiatric problems. Pazder claimed that he had been able to use hypnosis to reveal a long string of repressed memories from Michelle's childhood. Given the nature of these memories, it's no surprise that someone might want to repress them. Michelle told Pazder that she had been subject to routine physical and sexual abuse at the hands of her mother and a Satanic cult to which she belonged. The abuse was supposed to have begun in the early 1950s and continued for a number of years. Michelle's story includes incredibly graphic and upsetting rites involving ritual sacrifice, rape, murder, and basically anything unpleasant you can think of. It is unsurprising, then, that these claims captured the imagination of the public, horrified at the thought that such things could be going on right under their noses, in their own neighborhoods. Incredible as the claims seemed, people were willing to believe them, and the book set off a series of investigations into similar allegations of Satanic abuse of America's children.

Michelle's story might seem believable to someone who only heard the headlines. Child abuse is certainly an unfortunate reality of life, and it did not take too much imagination to stretch the mundane sufferings of children into a ritualized form complete with Satanic symbolism. But a closer look into Pazder's claims reveals some cracks in his story that would force even the most credulous reader to raise an eyebrow. For example, Pazder claims that during one of these ceremonies, the Satanists actually summoned the Devil himself, who proceeded to erase all the physical scars Michelle would have suffered from the years of abuse, as well as her memory. Granted, some explanation would be needed as to why the adult Michelle exhibited no physical signs of the abuse she claimed to have suffered, but this seems a little too convenient, doesn't it? Pazder also claimed that Michelle's mother belonged to The Church of Satan, an organization that predated Christianity. It's hard to see how the worship of Satan could come before the first religion to really develop the character as an idea, though, and in any case the only documented Church of Satan was founded in America by Anton LaVey in America a decade after Michelle's abuse was alleged to have occurred.

Unsurprisingly, independent investigators were able to uncover no corroborating evidence of Michelle's story, nor that a cult such as the one she described ever existed. Contrary to what the bored suburban imagination might suppose, it is not exactly easy to get away with blood sacrifice and ritual abuse on a regular basis without leaving some traces of your work behind, and it is difficult to believe that any such organization could operate for any length of time without the authorities getting wind of it.

In short, all serious people who looked into Michelle's story were forced to conclude that it was mostly, if not entirely, untrue. What actually happened between Pazder and his patient is unclear, but it could have consisted of a number of things. Perhaps he and Michelle deliberately concocted the story to gain publicity and money (it is worth noting here that Pazder later married Michelle, which says something about his sense of professional ethics, as well as suggesting something about their relationship as doctor and patient). Alternatively, Michelle could have made up the story herself, duping the credulous psychiatrist into going along with it. The most troubling possibility, which also seems the most likely given the stories to follow in this chapter, is that the memories of Satanic abuse were real, although the events themselves were not. In other words, Pazder might have implanted the memories into Michelle's mind using a combination of hypnosis and repeated suggestion to a woman in a vulnerable state. While this may sound like something out of a science fiction movie, human memory, especially in children or victims of trauma, is incredibly susceptible to suggestion and manipulation. This is part of why confessions in criminal trials are not regarded as conclusive evidence. It's not very difficult to persuade someone that they did something wrong if you press them long enough and hard enough under stressful conditions.

Suggestion by authority figures to create false memories played a major role in criminal charges that emerged after Pazder's book and lit a fire under law enforcement to uncover and prosecute Satanic cults.

Won't Someone Please Think of the Children?

As with most moral panics, the Satanic Panic relied heavily on concern for the most innocent and vulnerable members of the population, the children. At the start of the 1980s, more women were entering the workforce, resulting in the need for a greater reliance on child care professionals outside the home. Children too young to attend school would therefore be entrusted to day care centers while mommies and daddies went off to bring home the bacon. Naturally, this change in the family dynamic resulted in a fair amount of stress as mothers had to get used to the idea of entrusting their infants or toddlers to strangers. This anxiety fit in nicely with the urban legends about Satanic cults beginning to circulate, and of course books like *Michelle Remembers*.

In fact, that book was specifically used as training material for social workers in Kern County, California, the site of the initial accusations of Satanic ritual abuse that would soon become a nationwide witch hunt. In 1982, children in Kern county began to come forward with wild claims about a Satanic pedophilia ring that ritually abused children. The initial accusations came from the two daughters of Alvin and Debbie McCuan. They claimed that their parents, along with others in the community had abused them, and other children backed up the claim. In 1984, the McCuan's were sentenced to life in prison, their case enthusiastically prosecuted by District Attorney Ed Jagels. Under Jagels' leadership, the state went on to convict 36 people of Satanic ritual abuse. There was never any physical evidence for the claims presented, just the testimony of the children. In the case of the McCuans, the children were later found to have been coached in their testimony with their step-grandmother, who had custody of the girls at the time. Other accusers later recanted their testimony, admitting that they made up the charges. Of the 36 convictions, 34 were later overturned on appeal, but not before some of the accused had spent decades in prison for crimes they didn't commit. The remaining two convictions could not be overturned because the accused parties had already died in prison. Jagels, the man responsible for the wrongful convictions, continued to serve as District Attorney until 2009.

In 1983, a mother named Judy Johnson brought allegations that teachers at Virginia McMartin's preschool in Manhattan Beach, California had sexually abused her son. As part of the investigation, police sent a letter to some 200 parents asking them to question their children about potential abuse from teachers at the school. The children were then interviewed by staff at a local therapy clinic specializing in abuse. In addition to allegations about abuse, statements from the children contained improbable tales about seeing witches fly and traveling through a complex network of tunnels below the school.

After a trial that lasted seven years and would go down as the longest and most expensive in the U.S. to that date, the accused teachers were either acquitted or their charges dismissed. This nevertheless resulted in teachers being held in jail for years without ever being convicted of a crime, their reputations ruined.

But what about the children's testimony? Why did they all report abuse when none had apparently occurred? Review of the interview tapes revealed that interviews used extremely coercive and leading questions to get the answers they wanted from the children. As anyone who has dealt with young children can tell you, they are generally more eager to get the "right" or expected answer in order to please authority figures than to stick to the truth at all costs. They are susceptible to leading questions and implanted suggestions, and if they are questioned repeatedly about the same topic, they will tend to change their answer, believing that the initial response must have been incorrect. Instead of asking open-ended questions like "what happened?" the interviewers tended to rely on questions that themselves contained the desired answer, for example "he touched you, didn't he?" or "where did he touch you?"

Years later, one of the children who had made accusations of abuse recanted her earlier claims, and expressed remorse for what he had done.

Never did anyone do anything to me, and I never saw them doing anything. I said a lot of things that didn't happen. I lied. ... Anytime I would give them an answer that they didn't like, they would ask again and encourage me to give them the answer they were looking for. ... I felt uncomfortable and a little ashamed that I was being dishonest. But at the same time, being the type of person I was, whatever my parents wanted me to do, I would do.[47]

It is also worth noting that the authors of *Michelle Remembers* met with many of the parents and children before the trial, two people with a clear incentive to influence the testimony in favor of abuse. As for Judy Johnson, the woman who made the initial allegations, she was later hospitalized with paranoid schizophrenia and alcoholism, and was revealed to have faced a long-term struggle with mental illness. This gives some context to her bizarre insistence that the teachers abusing her son were also able to fly.

Some of the parents in the McMartin case founded an organization called Believe the Children, in order to continue to push the idea that Satanic ritual abuse is real and not simply a product of mass hysteria. The organization assisted in the prosecution of Dan and Fran Keller, who ran a small daycare in Austin, Texas. In 1991, the Kellers were accused of abusing many of the children in their charge, donning white robes, lighting candles, serving the children blood-laced Kool-Aid, and conducting a wide variety of abuse, including the children as well as to animals. Despite a lack of physical evidence, the Kellers were sentenced to 48 years in prison. The couple were released in 2013 following a reevaluation of the case. The prosecution was discovered to have engaged in numerous forms of misconduct, which cast doubt on the legitimacy of the trial. In 2017, the Kellers were declared "actually innocent" and all charges against them were dismissed.

These are just the most high-profile cases and, in fact, many other day care facilities were charged with child abuse during this period. Of course, it is possible that some of the charges may have been justified, but the tendency of accusers to imagine outlandish Satanic rituals and supernatural powers, and the willingness of court rooms to give credence to these charges, says a lot about the hysterical state of the country at that time.

The 1980s was a time of great change, where the country was seeing new forms of entertainment, new music, new ways of dressing and acting, and new dynamics in the workforce and family. Change is usually met with fear and a lack of understanding, but not generally to such an exaggerated extent. Nonconformists in the form of role players, metal heads, Goths, and day care operators were not only resisted, they were labeled as literal allies of the Devil, and persecuted as such. This persecution ranged from simply harassment and social stigma to using the court system to destroy people's entire lives, all over some ridiculously overblown fears about Satan lurking behind every corner. Like the Salem Witch Trials before it, the Satanic Panic should serve as a reminder to all of us how badly fear can get out of control, and the devastating effects it can have on the lives and livelihoods of ordinary citizens.

Much of the material for this chapter was sourced from a lecture delivered by Seth Andrews at the Florida Freethought Convention on October 22, 2017, entitled "The Satanic Panic: The Witch Hunt of the Late 20th Century". The lecture is available on YouTube, and I highly recommend it to anyone who wants to learn more about this troubling period in our history.

Chapter 9

Modern Demons

The persecution of nonconformists in general is a broad enough topic that I wanted to narrow it down to something more specific, as well as something that other authors have not spent much time examining. I therefore chose to focus on the ways in which free thinkers have been *literally* demonized throughout the years. Where does that leave us today, though? As a progressive, western, materialistic society, we no longer believe in demons, despite what the continued popularity of films like *The Exorcist* and its legion of imitators would indicate. Certainly, you can still find plenty of Christians who profess a belief in the Devil or his equivalent, but in general these beliefs have been trending towards something more metaphorical in nature. I don't expect too many people actually blame honest-to-god demons for the actions of criminals or mental patients, and for many years the Catholic Church has shown an extreme reluctance to perform exorcisms, even when asked to do so by desperate parishioners, fearing embarrassment.

At least, this is the perception most of us have. In fact, official polling data paints a somewhat different picture. According to Gallup, 70 percent of Americans believed in the Devil in 2007. That seems high, but if we interpret the question to mean some immaterial force for evil rather than a goat-like figure with a tail and a pitchfork, it's not too surprising. However, a 2013 survey by YouGov offers some further insights into American belief that might be more startling. In contrast to Gallup, YouGov put belief in the Devil at only 57 percent, but 51 percent admitted to the possibility of demonic possession. While 28 percent denied a belief in possession, when asked how often possessions occur, only 11 percent said "never", while 15 percent said "frequently" or "very frequently". While the Church doesn't publish any official statistics on exorcisms, anecdotal evidence collected for an article in *The Atlantic* found that demand for exorcisms is on the rise, with the official exorcist of Indianapolis admitting to receiving more than 1,700 requests for exorcisms in the year 2018 alone. The article also claims that the Church has been ramping up the training of new exorcists, presumably in response to the swell in demand.

What do these numbers mean for the ongoing demonization of nonconformists? Possibly not much. In spite of occasional flare ups, the Satanic Panic seems to be well and truly over. Newspaper headlines are not dominated by outrageous claims of human sacrifice and dark magic rituals, although I can think of at least one fairly high-profile case of Satanic hysteria in the last few years.

During the 2016 presidential election, an online conspiracy theory that became known as "pizzagate" gained some prominence. Believers began alleging that high-ranking members of the Democratic Party, including then-presidential candidate Hillary Clinton, were involved in a massive pedophilia and human trafficking ring, and that they practiced Satanic ritual abuse on captured children. For some reason, the headquarters for this ring was said to be Comet Ping Pong, a Washington, DC area pizzeria, hence the name. Thankfully, this obvious nonsense was quickly debunked and dismissed by anyone of importance. It would appear that the repeated wolf-crying over the Satanic Panic has at least left people with a protective layer of skepticism when it comes to accusations of Satanism.

By now, pizzagate has mostly been forgotten, although remnants of the conspiracy theory still occasionally crop up elsewhere in the dark recesses of the internet, such as in the conspiracy group Q. Fortunately, it appears that nobody is prepared to take these people seriously, at least not at this time.

In spite of the relative infrequency of Satanic or demonic

accusations, and a higher level of public skepticism regarding such claims, it would be a mistake to assume that we have entered a golden age of tolerance in which the nonconformist is free to practice his alternative lifestyle or belief system without fear of persecution.

Diversity Is Our Strength

One of the ironies of twenty-first century America is that, while diversity is aggressively championed as a *sine qua non* of a civilized, inclusive society, nonconformity is still heavily frowned upon, even aggressively shouted down by the academic left. Racial minorities, ethnic minorities, people with minority gender identities or sexual preferences are all considered worthy of protection, which of course they are, but minority opinion, especially on topics of politics, economics, sociology, psychology, ecology, and even philosophy are liable to get one in serious hot water.

Multiple social scientists have released papers claiming that conservative or "right wing" ideology should actually be classified as a mental disorder or a neurological defect. The goal, particularly given that social science professors are overwhelmingly left wing, is to delegitimize dissenting opinions. It is not merely that the other side has a disagreement involving facts or values; it is that there is actually *something wrong with them*. And if conservatism is a disease, it can be written off in the same way that people's messiah complexes and delusions of persecution can be written off. Moreover, if right wing views are the product of a disease, then maybe they can be "cured" in much the same way that psychiatrists once tried to "cure" homosexuality: through medication, public shaming, and torture. It is all part of the effort to annihilate diversity of opinion while promoting diversity of superficial factors like skin color.

I don't wish to dwell on this point lest I risk turning this book into a polemic, but I do think that it is worth acknowledging the inconsistency here. Of course, some opinions should be condemned by all decent human beings, and I would not want my words to be interpreted as a defense of pure moral relativism or undiscriminating tolerance for evil. On the other hand, if the previous pages have taught us anything, it's that bad things can happen when moral certainty becomes too rigid. Such an attitude risks replacing critical thought and sensible moral judgements with unyielding dogmatism, under which heretics must be unmasked and punished at any cost. I'm sure you can think of a few modern heresies without me having to point them out to you, and the era of social media shaming, in which every careless word or deed is preserved for posterity to judge, has left behind it a trail of lives destroyed.

There is, however, one thing the advocates for diversity get right, and that is the danger of racism and xenophobia. If the left tends to demonize conservatives for their values and views on the economy, the right is too often guilty of demonizing "the other" in the form of foreign workers. Part of this stems from legitimate economic anxiety. Foreign workers represent more competition, meaning that some Americans will have to work harder at lower wages in order to keep up. It's understandable why someone, particularly in a field already threatened by outsourcing, such as the automobile industry, would resent these competitors. Without wishing to enter into an in-depth discussion of immigration policy, it is worth pointing out that the downside to the individual worker is generally counterbalanced by the contributions of foreign workers to society in the form of lower prices for consumers, more brains in the country capable of solving problems and innovating, and the simple fact that more workers means more work gets done. Still, it's cold comfort to an out of work factory worker to know that his neighbors will enjoy a discount on spark plugs from now on.

There is another element of xenophobia, however, that is less easy to rationalize, and that is the vague fear that "the culture" is threatened by admitting workers and refugees from other countries. In the first place, whatever common culture America has is an amalgamation of a diverse citizenry with origins stretching around the globe. Halloween comes from Ireland, Christmas trees from Germany, pizza from Italy, and the language from England. The cartoons children watch are influenced by Japanese culture, surfing came from the South Pacific, hamburgers and hot dogs are, again, German, and baseball, that all American pastime, was first described in a novel by English writer Jane Austen. California would not be the same without China's influence, New Orleans would not exist without the French, that charming Midwestern accent found in Minnesota and upper Michigan comes from Scandinavia, and Texas is packed with Mexican culture.

At the end of the day "the culture" is just what people choose to do, what they eat, how they dress, and the celebrations they engage in together. There's no reason why you should have to fear the disappearance of Christmas or Easter just because someone of a different religion moves in down the street. If the preceding pages have taught us anything it's that religious freedom is a cornerstone of individual liberty, and it's not strengthened by shunning or outlawing the practices of people from diffident cultures.

Cancel Culture: Heresy for the Twenty-First Century

The demand for uniformity of opinion in the public sphere resulted in an interesting—and disturbing—phenomenon. Cancel culture holds that it's not enough to respond to, criticize, debate, rebut, and condemn opinions with which we disagree; anyone who expresses those opinions must be harassed, boycotted, stripped of their livelihood, and driven from public life, often under the overt threat of violence.

While free speech continues to be protected in the United States, to the extent that the government cannot actually prosecute you for what you say, hate speech laws have become popular in other countries, meaning a controversial opinion could land you in jail. Similar policies have cropped up on college campuses, corporate boardrooms, and across social media platforms. While you may not face jail time for saying something a bit rude, you can certainly lose your job, be expelled from college, and be denied a platform with which to communicate with the world at large. As I write this, author J.K. Rowling is facing aggressive attacks over her controversial claim that women menstruate, a New York Times editor has been fired for running an op-ed piece from a prominent senator, there are calls for Twitter to ban the account of the President of the United States, and podcaster Dave Rubin has faced such problems with deplatforming on existing sites that he has gone off and started his own. In Rowling's case, there is a certain unpleasant irony in the fact that she has seamlessly transitioned from condemnation by the religious right for her alleged promotion of witchcraft, to condemnation from the progressive left for holding "incorrect" views on gender and sex. This poor woman can't catch a break, and I would feel bad for her if it were not for the solace she no doubt gets from her billion-dollar bank account.

This is just a snapshot in time, out of date as soon as I write it, but it may serve to give you a sense that the concept of heresy is still very much alive and well. The practice of shunning and banishing the offending party from the community recalls very clearly the superstition of the scapegoat discussed in Chapter 1. The offending creature must be sent away from the tribe, in the hope that the burden of sin will go with it, never to return.

The orthodox positions on race, gender, climate science, and a host of other issues are not to be questioned, just as the orthodox position on a geocentric universe was once not to be questioned. As we have seen in previous chapters, progress only comes about through upsetting the status quo, asking uncomfortable questions, and giving men of genius enough latitude to explore new ideas. When new ideas are outlawed, society stagnates, sinking into a putrid mire of superstition and fear.

That is not to say that I think these orthodox positions are *wrong*. Some I agree with, some I dispute, and some I think are basically right but with some complicating factors. But being right or wrong is not the point. The point is being able to ask questions in the first place, for questioning and testing, again and again, is the only way to distinguish what is true from what is false.

Today, some people lament the advent of "fake news". There are now so many news sources, so easily accessible, and with such conflicting viewpoints that it is difficult to sort fact from fiction. It was better, they argue, when there was only one news source; that way you could trust the information you heard. The argument is a fallacious one. Having only a single news source may eliminate doubt from the minds of the credulous, and they may find some comfort in that lack of doubt, but there is no reason to assume that the stories presented by a single news source were any truer than those being peddled today on the fringes of the internet. The only difference is that there was no one to detect and call out lies and misinformation when they occurred. Today's chaotic web of conflicting news sources may be confusing, but it allows for a system of checks and balances to challenge misinformation and present alternative viewpoints. Sorting through the noise to find the truth may be difficult at times, but at least we have that option. In the absence of competing voices, we are left with a single authority insisting that the Earth is the center of the universe, and anyone who says otherwise can go straight to jail.

The Ultimate Rebellion

While western society has admittedly become more tolerant over the years, there remains one act that cuts so sharply against established norms, and which represents such a departure from the way most people think that we continue to regard it with uncomprehending horror. It is the ultimate act of nonconformity, a rebellion against life itself. I'm speaking, of course, about the act of taking one's own life.

It is commonly asserted that society is more sharply divided on questions of values than ever before, resulting in a polarization that makes cooperation and even civil discourse nearly impossible in many cases. In some ways, this is probably true, but there is one value on which the vast majority of people strongly agree: the idea that life is good and therefore must be continued for as long as possible, at nearly any cost. We often hear politicians earnestly justifying some new policy, dismissing any concerns about potential downsides or tradeoffs with the platitude that it will be worth it "if it saves just one life." Of course, even the most cursory inspection reveals the absurdity of such a statement. People die in car accidents, in organized sports, in swimming pools, from falling off ladders or down staircases, from electric shocks, from eating unhealthy food, from drinking, from smoking, and from crossing the road. People are killed by falling trees, animal attacks, plane crashes, sexually transmitted diseases, and accidental suffocation. The amount of lives we could save by taking swift and decisive action to ban cars, planes, pools, sports, pets, stairs, hamburgers, sex, beer, cigarettes, electricity, and pillows is incalculable. The reason we don't ban those things comes from a recognition that life is inherently risky, and a life which minimized every conceivable danger would not be one worth living.

The person who chooses to commit suicide has made a calculation that life, at least in his own case, is *not* worth living, and that the pain of existence is less desirable even than oblivion, or whatever else lies beyond. For many, this calculation is so inconceivable that, rather than confront it, it is easier to deny its existence. Suicidal persons, we are told, are *not* making a rational decision to end their lives. Instead, they are victims of a disease, a mental illness, they are not in control of their actions, their brains not capable of forming a rational thought. They are, by definition, insane.

In the opening of his lengthy treatment of the subject of suicide, Thomas Szasz puts his finger on society's apprehensions about suicide as an act of nonconformity:

Although most people are squeamish about dying, nearly everyone accepts death due to old age, disease, accident, and even murder as understandable or "normal." Suicide is a different matter: Killing oneself is generally viewed with abhorrence (sometimes reverence) and the act of deliberately causing one's own death is treated as spooky, defying understanding, something "abnormal" or better not spoken or thought about. According to a 1992 poll, 71 percent of Americans want libraries to ban books "describing how to commit suicide."[48]

It's a puzzling attitude when you consider that most of us do things to hasten our demise on a daily basis. As mentioned above, virtually every action you take has a chance, sometimes approaching certainty, of shortening your life. Death is not optional. It *will* come for all of us at some point. The suicidal person is not choosing *to* die; he's going to die anyway. He's choosing *when* to die, and under what circumstances. Looked at in this way, what is the moral difference between a person who kills himself over the course of twenty years of hard drinking and the person who kills himself over the course a few hours, having ingested sleeping pills?

Two characteristics of twenty-first century American culture are a preoccupation with health, both physical and mental, and an overwhelming desire to delegate decision making authority to experts. The health obsession makes this fear of suicide understandable. What could be less healthy than voluntarily ending one's own life? It may also explain why the Centers for Disease Control and Prevention devote a considerable amount of their resources to the problem of suicide, despite it quite obviously not being a disease, but rather an action deliberately taken. Older civilizations, such as the Romans and Greeks, did not express the same religious awe towards suicide as we do, but neither did they conceptualize bodily health as the highest possible moral good.

The tendency to rely on experts explains why, although suicide remains an all but unbreakable taboo, the practice of euthanasia has steadily become more socially acceptable. If a doctor gives his professional opinion that a patient should die, that is one thing; if the patient autonomously decides to die, it is another. The former situation conforms with social norms about deferring to authority and following the advice of others, while the other represents a stubborn defiance of convention, as well as disregard for the wishes of friends and family.

Ethically, euthanasia is a considerably more complicated subject than that of suicide, as it involves the deliberate and premeditated killing of one human being by another (usually classified as murder by most courts of law). Suicide, on the other hand, involves only one person acting upon his or her own body. This is not the place for an in-depth discussion of the ethics of euthanasia, however. It remains sufficient to point out that the act of rebellion against an undesired life remains the subject of much instinctual revulsion and demonization.

The Counter-Revolution in Zombies

We have seen that most of recorded history has been characterized by a fear that the individualist poses a threat to the group, and the often extreme measures taken to hammer down the nail that dares to stick out. For a brief period of time, however, the opposite phenomenon could be observed, providing an extremely interesting and telling contrast to the central thesis of this book.

For much of the twentieth century America, along with other western nations, lived in intense fear of the Communist menace. The sudden rise of the Soviet Union, Maoist China, Pol Pot's Khmer Rouge in Cambodia and the dominance of communists in North Vietnam made it appear as though this new ideology would rapidly devour the globe, and the western way of life with it.

Communism is a fundamentally collectivist philosophy. The needs of the individual, the family, and the company were all to be subjugated before the needs of the Party, or in other words, the aims of international communism writ large. Even the nation itself was regarded as less important than the global collective communism hoped to create, and this in part was what created the sharp divisions between the communists and the fascists, two basically collectivist groups that have more in common than most historians would have you believe.

During the Cold War, the triumph of communism along with its implications of destroying individual identity became a major source of anxiety in the West, and we can see this anxiety manifested in popular culture. In *Star Trek: The Next Generation*, the 1980s retooling of Gene Roddenberry's techno-optimist vision of the future, an intrepid crew of space cowboys is confronted with the chilling alien life form known as The Borg. Much like an insect colony, the Borg is a hive mind in which individual members have no value except in their ability to serve the group. Indeed, they have no distinct personalities or personal wills at all, and instead function more like appendages to a larger body. The Borg were frightening, alien, incomprehensible, unsympathetic, and relentless. A less subtle allegory for communism as perceived by the West would be hard to come by.

As popular as Star Trek remains, however, there exists a cultural critique of mindless conformity that is even more enduring: the Zombie Movie. In a trend kicked off by Italian filmmaker George Romero's sensational *Night of the Living Dead*, zombies quickly rose through the ranks of popular mythology to a status rivaling vampires, and arguably eclipsing such previous favorites as mummies, wolfmen, and Frankenstein monsters. Romero drew his source material from Haitian folklore, in which Voodoo priests could allegedly rob victims of their free will through magico-chemical means. The resulting shambling creatures were neither dead nor alive—the *un*dead—doomed to mindlessly carry out the will of their masters in the service of evil. Romero expanded on these legends, depicting a world in which ordinary people could be transformed into lurching, inhuman monstrosities through the spread of some mysterious pathogen. Depending on which film you watch, the condition may be spread through zombie bites, a kind of undead rabies, or through the same methods as an ordinary virus. Once infected, however, there was no going back for the unfortunate victim. He or she would lose all personality and fall in line with a horde of identical monsters, searching mindlessly for sustenance in the form of human flesh and, occasionally, *braaaiiinnnsss!*

At first glance, the popularity of zombies looks just like an extension of the phenomenon of older, Universal-style monster movies. As one type of creature went out of fashion, another came in. No big mystery there. But there is an important difference between the nature of zombies and their late-night horror predecessors. The films of the 1930s, Frankenstein, Dracula, the Wolfman, and so on, were largely based on characters and archetypes developed in the nineteenth century and earlier. Frankenstein and Dracula were novels written by nineteenth century authors, while folklore surrounding werewolves and vampires, as discussed in an earlier chapter, dates back hundreds of years. The vampire or werewolf is scary because he looks and behaves differently from ordinary people, and as such represents a threat to the status quo. Count Dracula is a nonconformist, refusing to abide by the social, and indeed legal, norms of his time. Victor Frankenstein is the modern Galileo, a lone and dangerous scientist delving into knowledge man was never meant to have. The fact that the subtitle of Mary Shelley's novel, too frequently forgotten today, is "A Modern Prometheus" tells you everything you need to know. Like the unfortunate Titan, Frankenstein brought new technology to the world, and was destroyed for his troubles. All of these movies, to which could be added The Invisible Man, the Creature from the Black Lagoon, King Kong, Dr. Jekyll and Mr. Hyde, The Phantom of the Opera, and dozens of others, point out implicitly the dangers of being different. The titular monsters are aberrations from the norm, and in almost every case the penalty for such deviance is death.

Zombies, however, are fundamentally different. Slow moving, mindless, and without any particularly mysterious powers or weapons, an individual zombie poses little threat to the population at large. A well-aimed gun, or even an axe, hammer, or bat, can destroy what's left of the creature's brain and render it quite harmless in a matter of seconds. No, the threat of zombies lies in their sheer numbers and ability to multiply. We don't fear the zombie as a minority, we fear that they might become the *majority*. The iconic image on many a zombie movie poster shows a lone man, hopelessly outnumbered by identical foes. The horror of zombies lies in the persecution of the individual by the collective, a perfect parallel to the way Americans thought about communism in the middle of the twentieth century. And as the Cold War waned, zombies began to take on new symbolism, popping up as critiques of other forms of collectivism, such as blind consumerism and unthinking obedience to political factions.

The popularity of zombie fiction shows that the human tendency to represent real-world anxieties in terms of supernatural evil cuts both ways, and that no one is immune from literal demonization. In 1954, the famed evangelical preacher Billy Graham denounced communism as "Satan's religion" and referred to communists as "disciples of Lucifer". Given the history outlined in the rest of this book, it's refreshing to see a religious leader stand up for individualism. On the other hand, Graham's reaction may have had more to do with the overt atheism and anti-theism of communist leaders than in a principled opposition to collectivism.

Still, the fact that the popularity of zombies in popular culture has proved so durable over the years may say something about an inherently American resistance to conformity. As pointed out in an earlier chapter, the original American colonists had to be nonconformists by definition in order to risk the ordeal of starting a new country from scratch. One would hope that a portion of that spirit remains, as reflected by such unlikely sources as The Walking Dead, World War Z, Zombieland, and a host of other franchises breathing new life into the idea that there's something deeply scary about mindlessly following the crowd.

In some sense, the nonconformists may always be doomed to garner reactions of hatred and fear from those that cannot or will not understand their unique point of view. On the other hand, perhaps there is room for optimism as well. As long as the stories we tell make villains of those who abandon reason and independence for the will of the collective, there is at least some hope for all the oddballs out there.

References

1   Thomas Karlsson, *Qabalah, Qliphoth and Goetic Magic*, p. 48, Ajna, Jacksonville, OR, 2019.

2   C.G. Jung, *Answer to Job*, p. 8, Princeton University Press, Princeton, NJ, 2002.

3   James George Frazer, *The Golden Bough: A Study of Magic and Religion*, pp. 669-670, Collier Books, Springfield, OH, 1963.

4   *Areopagitica and Other Political Writings of John Milton*, p. x, Liberty Fund, Indianapolis, IN, 1999.

5   Keith Wagstaff (2015) *Donald Trump Calls for 'Closing That Internet Up'* (online). Available at: https://www. nbcnews.com/tech/internet/donald-trump-calls-closing-internet-n476156 (Accessed 13 November 2020).

6   John Holt, *Escape From Childhood*, p. 55, HoltGWS LLC, Medford, MA, 2013.

7   Helmut Schoeck, *Envy: a Theory of Social Behaviour*, p. 3, Liberty Fund, Indianapolis, IN, 1987.

8   *Ibid.* p. 40.

9   Ayn Rand, *The Fountainhead*, pp. 736-737, Bobbs-Merrill, Indianapolis, IN, 1943.

10 Plato, *The Dialogues of Plato*, p. 203, Encyclopedia Britannica, Inc., Chicago, IL, 1952.

11 E.J. Holmyard, *Alchemy*, p. 231, Dover Publications, Mineola, NY, 1990.

12 2 Timothy 3:12

13 1 John 3:13

14 Matthew 5:10

15 Eliphas Levi, Magic: *A History of Its Rites and Rituals*, Footnote to p. 211, Dover Publications, Mineola, NY, 2006.

16 Thomas Keightley, *The Knights Templar and Other Secret Societies of the Middle Ages*, p. 239, Dover Publications,

Mineola, NY, 2007.

17 John Michael Greer, *The Conspiracy Book,* p. 9, Sterling Publishing, New York, NY, 2018.

18 Gareth Knight, *A History of White Magic,* p. 100, Skylight Press, Cheltenham, Glos, 2011.

19 Eliphas Levi, *Magic: A History of Its Rites and Rituals,* pp. 147-148, Dover Publications, Mineola, NY, 2006.

20 Exodus 22:18

21 Heinrich Kramer and James Sprenger (Montague Summers, trans.), *The Malleus Maleficarum,* p. xii, Dover Publications, Mineola, NY, 1971.

22 *Ibid.* p. 47.

23 *Ibid.* p. 41.

24 *Ibid.* p. 237.

25 *Ibid.* p. viii.

26 Rossell Hope Robbins, *The Encyclopedia of Witchcraft and Demonology,* p. 14, Crown Publishers, Inc., New York, NY, 1959.

27 *Ibid.* p. 432.

28 Charlotte F. Otten, ed., *A Lycanthropy Reader,* pp. 195-196, Syracuse University Press, Syracuse, NY, 1986.

29 Josh McDowell and Don Stewart, *The Occult: The Authority of the Believer Over the Powers of Darkness,* p. 206, Here's Life Publishers, Inc., San Bernardino, CA, 1992.

30 Thomas Szasz, *Fatal Freedom: The Ethics and Politics of Suicide,* p. 51, Syracuse University Press, Syracuse, NY, 1999.

31 Mark 5:3-5

32 Matthew 17:15

33 Mark 9:18

34 Matthew 12:22

35 Montague Summers, *The History of Witchcraft and Demonology,* pp. 205-206, Bristol Park Books, New York, NY, 2010.

36 Dion Fortune, *Psychic Self-Defense,* pp. 69-70, Red Wheel/

Weiser, San Francisco, CA, 2001.

37 Thomas Szasz, *The Manufacture of Madness*, p. 5, Syracuse University Press, Syracuse, NY, 1997.

38 *Ibid.* p. 13.

39 Anthony Storr, *Solitude: A Return to the Self*, pp. 166-167, Ballantine Books, New York, NY, 1989.

40 Ann Braude, *Radical Spirits*, p. 82, Indiana University Press, Bloomington, IN, 2001.

41 Montague Summers, *The History of Witchcraft and Demonology*, pp. 268-269, Bristol Park Books, New York, NY, 2010.

42 Ann Braude, *Radical Spirits*, p. 157, Indiana University Press, Bloomington, IN, 2001.

43 John Michael Greer, *The Conspiracy Book*, p. 43, Sterling Publishing, New York, NY, 2018.

44 Mark Rosewater (2004) *Where Have All the Demons Gone?* (online). Available at: https://magic.wizards.com/en/articles/archive/making-magic/where-have-all-demons-gone-2004-07-05 (Accessed 18 October 2020).

45 Josh McDowell and Don Stewart, *The Occult: The Authority of the Believer Over the Powers of Darkness*, p. 28, Here's Life Publishers, Inc., San Bernardino, CA, 1992.

46 Frederick Thomas Elworthy, *The Evil Eye: The Classic Account of an Ancient Superstition*, p. 261, Dover Publications, Mineola, NY, 2004.

47 Kyle Zirpolo (2005) *I'm Sorry* (online). Available at https://www.latimes.com/archives/la-xpm-2005-oct-30-tm-mcmartin44-story.html (Accessed 18 October 2020).

48 Thomas Szasz, *Fatal Freedom: The Ethics and Politics of Suicide*, p. 1, Syracuse University Press, Syracuse, NY, 1999.

Bibliography

Alexander, Lloyd, *The Chronicles of Prydain*

Augustine, *Confessions*

Barnstone, Willis & Marvin Meyer, Eds., *The Gnostic Bible*

Braude, Ann, *Radical Spirits*

Clarke, Arthur C., *Childhood's End*

Crowley, Aleister, *Magick in Theory and Practice*

Elworthy, Frederick Thomas, *The Evil Eye: The Classic Account of an Ancient Superstition*

Fortune, Dion, *Psychic Self-Defense*

Frazer, James George, *The Golden Bough: A Study of Magic and Religion*

Garry, Gemma, *Traditional Witchcraft*

Garry, Gemma, *The Devil's Dozen: Thirteen Craft Rites of the Old One*

Goethe, Johann Wolfgang von, *Faust*

Greer, John Michael, *The Conspiracy Book*

Hayek, Friedrich, *The Fatal Conceit*

Holmyard, E.J., *Alchemy*

Holt, John, *Escape From Childhood*

The Holy Bible

Jung, C.G., *Answer to Job*

Karlsson, Thomas, *Qabalah, Qliphoth and Goetic Magic*

Keightley, Thomas, *The Knights Templar and Other Secret Societies of the Middle Ages*

Knight, Gareth, *A History of White Magic*

Kramer, Heinrich and James Sprenger, *The Malleus Maleficarum*

LaVey, Anton, *The Satanic Bible*

Levi, Eliphas, *The Doctrine and Ritual of Transcendental Magic*

Levi, Eliphas, *Magic: A History of Its Rites and Rituals*

Marlowe, Christopher, *Dr. Faustus*

McDowell, Josh & Don Stewart, *The Occult: The Authority of the*

Believer Over the Powers of Darkness

Mead, G.R.S., *Simon Magus*

Milton, John, *Areopagitica and Other Political Writings*

Milton, John, *Paradise Lost*

Otten, Charlotte F. ed., *A Lycanthropy Reader*

Plato, *Apology*

Rand, Ayn, *The Fountainhead*

Rand, Ayn, *The Virtue of Selfishness*

Ridley, Matt, *How Innovation Works*

Robbins, Rossell Hope, *The Encyclopedia of Witchcraft and Demonology*

Schoeck, Helmut, *Envy*

Shelley, Mary, *Frankenstein*

Sitwell, Edith, *English Eccentrics*

Storr, Anthony, *Solitude: A Return to the Self*

Edward Stringham, ed., *Anarchy and the Law*

Summers, Montague, *The History of Witchcraft and Demonology*

Szasz, Thomas, *The Manufacture of Madness*

Szasz, Thomas, *Fatal Freedom*

Thoreau, Henry David, *Walden*

Tucker, Robert, *The Marx-Engels Reader*

Wilson, Colin, *The Occult*

Logan Albright is a writer, musician, libertarian, and occultist. His previous book, *Our Servants, Our Masters: How Control Masquerades as Assistance*, was an examination of the ways in which people and institutions use the language of compassion and service while actually seeking obedience and conformity. He is currently the head writer at Free the People Foundation as well as an initiate in the Firefly House in Washington, DC.

Any questions or comments about this book can be directed to logan.albright@gmail.com.

**MOON
BOOKS**

PAGANISM & SHAMANISM

What is Paganism? A religion, a spirituality, an alternative belief system, nature worship? You can find support for all these definitions (and many more) in dictionaries, encyclopaedias, and text books of religion, but subscribe to any one and the truth will evade you. Above all Paganism is a creative pursuit, an encounter with reality, an exploration of meaning and an expression of the soul. Druids, Heathens, Wiccans and others, all contribute their insights and literary riches to the Pagan tradition. Moon Books invites you to begin or to deepen your own encounter, right here, right now. If you have enjoyed this book, why not tell other readers by posting a review on your preferred book site.

Recent bestsellers from Moon Books are:

Journey to the Dark Goddess
How to Return to Your Soul
Jane Meredith
Discover the powerful secrets of the Dark Goddess and transform your depression, grief and pain into healing and integration.
Paperback: 978-1-84694-677-6 ebook: 978-1-78099-223-5

Shamanic Reiki
Expanded Ways of Working with Universal Life Force Energy
Llyn Roberts, Robert Levy
Shamanism and Reiki are each powerful ways of healing; together,

their power multiplies. *Shamanic Reiki* introduces techniques to help healers and Reiki practitioners tap ancient healing wisdom.
Paperback: 978-1-84694-037-8 ebook: 978-1-84694-650-9

Pagan Portals – The Awen Alone
Walking the Path of the Solitary Druid
Joanna van der Hoeven
An introductory guide for the solitary Druid, *The Awen Alone* will accompany you as you explore, and seek out your own place within the natural world.
Paperback: 978-1-78279-547-6 ebook: 978-1-78279-546-9

A Kitchen Witch's World of Magical Herbs & Plants
Rachel Patterson
A journey into the magical world of herbs and plants, filled with magical uses, folklore, history and practical magic. By popular writer, blogger and kitchen witch, Tansy Firedragon.
Paperback: 978-1-78279-621-3 ebook: 978-1-78279-620-6

Medicine for the Soul
The Complete Book of Shamanic Healing
Ross Heaven
All you will ever need to know about shamanic healing and how to become your own shaman…
Paperback: 978-1-78099-419-2 ebook: 978-1-78099-420-8

Shaman Pathways – The Druid Shaman
Exploring the Celtic Otherworld
Danu Forest
A practical guide to Celtic shamanism with exercises and techniques as well as traditional lore for exploring the Celtic Otherworld.
Paperback: 978-1-78099-615-8 ebook: 978-1-78099-616-5

Traditional Witchcraft for the Woods and Forests
A Witch's Guide to the Woodland with Guided Meditations and
Pathworking
Mélusine Draco
A Witch's guide to walking alone in the woods, with guided
meditations and pathworking.
Paperback: 978-1-84694-803-9 ebook: 978-1-84694-804-6

Naming the Goddess
Trevor Greenfield
Naming the Goddess is written by over eighty adherents and
scholars of Goddess and Goddess Spirituality.
Paperback: 978-1-78279-476-9 ebook: 978-1-78279-475-2

Shapeshifting into Higher Consciousness
Heal and Transform Yourself and Our World with Ancient
Shamanic and Modern Methods
Llyn Roberts
Ancient and modern methods that you can use every day to
transform yourself and make a positive difference in the world.
Paperback: 978-1-84694-843-5 ebook: 978-1-84694-844-2

Readers of ebooks can buy or view any of these bestsellers by
clicking on the live link in the title. Most titles are published in
paperback and as an ebook. Paperbacks are available in traditional
bookshops. Both print and ebook formats are available online.

Find more titles and sign up to our readers' newsletter at
http://www.johnhuntpublishing.com/paganism
Follow us on Facebook at https://www.facebook.com/MoonBooks
and Twitter at https://twitter.com/MoonBooksJHP